Speaking about the Unspeakable

by the same author

"If You Turned into a Monster"
Transformation through Play: A Body-Centred Approach to Play Therapy
Foreword by Richmond Greene
ISBN 978 1 84310 529 9

of related interest

Narrative Approaches in Play with Children
Ann Cattanach
ISBN 978 1 84310 588 6

Healing the Inner City Child
Creative Arts Therapies with At-Risk Youth
Edited by Vanessa A. Camilleri
ISBN 978 1 84310 824 5

Play Therapy with Abused Children
2nd edition
Ann Cattanach
ISBN 978 1 84310 587 9

Empowering Children through Art and Expression
Culturally Sensitive Ways of Healing Trauma and Grief
Bruce St Thomas and Paul Johnson
ISBN 978 1 84310 789 7

Replays
Using Play to Enhance Emotional and Behavioral Development
for Children with Autism Spectrum Disorders
Karen Levine and Naomi Chedd
ISBN 978 1 84310 832 0

Speaking about the Unspeakable

Non-Verbal Methods and Experiences in Therapy with Children

Edited by Dennis McCarthy

Foreword by Priscilla Rodgers

Jessica Kingsley Publishers
London and Philadelphia

'Last Night They Came' by David Whyte from *Where Many Rivers Meet* (1990) by David Whyte.
Printed with permission from Many Rivers Press, Langley, Washington. www.davidwhyte.com

First published in 2008
by Jessica Kingsley Publishers
116 Pentonville Road
London N1 9JB, UK
and
400 Market Street, Suite 400
Philadelphia, PA 19106, USA

www.jkp.com

Library of Congress Cataloging in Publication Data
Speaking about the unspeakable : non-verbal methods and experiences in therapy with children /
edited by Dennis McCarthy ; foreword by Priscilla Rodgers.
p. ; cm.
ISBN 978-1-84310-879-5 (pb : alk. paper) 1. Child psychotherapy. 2. Nonverbal communica-
tion in children. I. McCarthy, Dennis, 1951-
[DNLM: 1. Nonverbal Communication—psychology. 2. Play Therapy—methods. 3. Child.
WS 350.2 S741 2008]
RJ504.S587 2008
618.92'8914—dc22

2007048342

British Library Cataloguing in Publication Data
A CIP catalogue record for this book is available from the British Library

ISBN 978 1 84310 879 5

This book is dedicated to creative therapists around the world who are attempting in their work with children to listen and respond to the seemingly unspeakable language of the heart.

*"The creation of something new is not accomplished by
the intellect but by the play instinct acting from inner necessity."*

Carl Jung

Contents

FOREWORD   9
Priscilla Rodgers, Jungian analyst, NY

Introduction   11
Dennis McCarthy, Metamorfos Institute, NY

Chapter 1.   The Hidden Treasure of the Self   17
Jenny Bates, licensed clinical social worker in private practice, NY

Chapter 2.   Getting the Inside Out: Speaking with Clay   27
Michelle Rhodes, clay artist and art psychotherapist in private practice, NY

Chapter 3.   Speaking with the Body: Using Dance/Movement Therapy to Enhance Communication and Healing with Young Children   45
Claire LeMessurier, Children's Upstream Services, VT and Susan Loman, Antioch University, NH

Chapter 4.   Speaking with Silence: Play Therapy with Selective Mute Children   60
Brenda Lawrence, licensed clinical social worker, play therapist, and clay artist, Anguilla, West Indies

Chapter 5.   The Secret Garden: Healing through Nature   76
Ilka List, licensed creative arts therapist, NY

Chapter 6.   Speaking with the Imagination   89
Patti Knoblauch, psychologist in private practice, NY

Chapter 7.   Dance/Movement Therapy with Children   100
Rena Kornblum, Hancock Center for Dance/Movement Therapy Inc., WI

Chapter 8.   The Healing Power of Creative Expression   115
Nancy Mangano Rowe, Institute for Transpersonal Psychology, CA

Chapter 9.   Getting to the Core: Moving through the Language Barrier   130
Noelle Ghnassia Damon, licensed psychotherapist and certified EMDA practitioner in private practice, NY

Chapter 10.   Quicksand! Provocation to Change   143
Dennis McCarthy

Epilogue   151
Dennis McCarthy

CONTRIBUTORS   155

SUBJECT INDEX   158

AUTHOR INDEX   160

Last night they came with news of death
not knowing what I would say.

I wanted to say,
"The green wind is running through the fields,
making the grass lie flat."

I wanted to say,
"The apple blossom flakes like ash,
covering the orchard wall."

I wanted to say,
"The fish float belly up in the slow stream,
stepping stones to the dead."

They asked if I would sleep that night,
I said I did not know.

For this loss I could not speak,
the tongue lay idle in a great darkness,
the heart was strangely open,
the moon had gone,
and it was then
when I said, "He is no longer here",
that the night put its arms around me
and all the white stars turned bitter with grief.

David Whyte

Foreword

That which lives and moves human life is at its deepest core unspeakable. And, it would seem, the human imagination has evolved as the organ of communion with the unspeakable, for good and ill. It animates, plays with, disguises, expresses, dreams, falsifies, reveals and, most of all, gives form to what defies form or word. Yet engaging the power of the imagination to recreate a world torn apart is a rare art in these times.

The ancients, living in a dangerous world of presences, spirits, and crisis, responded by ritually telling and retelling, fashioning and refashioning their stories of creation in voice, art, song, and movement. Thus their arts made their world and their myths and created their reality in a way we would recognize today as psychological and emotional therapeutics applied to the human soul in the world. Without this, the human soul is torn from its world and the world itself is torn and dangerously unbalanced. This healing and creating process, so much a part of our heritage, is innate to humankind, but the movement of that process from collective ritual and religion to individual psyches and souls has been treacherous. The healing powers of the imagination have been eclipsed by the more shaded powers of artifice and advertising, model and media.

However, this book bears witness to the fact that imagination indeed lives next to and in league with that which troubles us, and also that it can and must be the heart of healing and renewal. This is an inspiring book. We as readers bear witness to several instances of a child finding his or her way through a traumatized and broken inner world to a place of most intimate and poignant healing by innately following a thread given by the heart and imagination in the presence of a gifted therapist. It would seem that the two-million-year-old man, of whom Jung speaks, is alive and well in even the most wounded child, and can still bring ancient and wise ways to bear. Without romanticizing the time of childhood, or the aliveness of the inner world of children, it is safe to say that the children spoken of in these pages are putting their lives back together and it is profoundly moving to see how very close the way through is for each of them once touched. We always imagine we are so very far away from what we need when we suffer trauma and that the solution is impossible. These children, struggling under often unbearable pain, seem to know in some also unspeakable way, exactly what they need to make or express in order to "speak" about what has not been able to be said or known. They dive in and bring about a great story of drama and form that is capable of ferrying them to the other side of trauma. When they are finished, they know they can move forward free from paralyzing trouble. Being reminded that we have evolved an imagination capable of this is inspiring.

Art-making of all kinds establishes an inner witness. This is, in part, why the creative process is experienced as healing. The witness is an additional position from which we can see, free from identification with the literal. It is part of what happens naturally when we engage in any art form. While we are making we are watching and witnessing what comes forth and we are bringing it together with what we feel and experience moment to moment. Often, and importantly so, this happens subliminally enough to skirt the judging, limiting, knowing, and fearing qualities of ego.

In this book, what is particularly moving in each case is the quality of witness each therapist brings to the encounter, creating a safe place for witnessing to occur. In so many places the therapists speak of needing to make little or no verbal or active intervention during the essentially non-verbal therapy. As the children create, each process proceeds inside a profound quality of witness and abiding engagement, bypassing the necessity of much, if any, interpretation. In their wisdom, the therapists hold the emotional charges and tensions of the unspoken so the imagination can sustain a symbolic function and bring about healing. We know the imagination can just as well serve to delude and falsify as it can heal. This quality of witness, coupled with the containing and suggestive qualities of the various art media and forms, attracts the imagination toward manifesting healing symbols and experience.

There are unspeakable places in each of us, and perhaps children living within these silences. Though we may not as adults have as unfettered an access to the dimension of the imagination as we may have had as children, we can learn this route to the unspeakable parts of ourselves and walk thus alongside our worded ways to our great benefit. In witnessing these children's lives we can support and sustain the undeniable powers of the imagination to bring about transformative change. We can perhaps be inspired to be fearless and open enough to engage in this rare and endangered art. In so doing we may resuscitate our world, even a little, as she glides along in a dark night amidst the many unspeakable horrors we make together, seeming to have lost her way to see through, to, and by way of the imagination.

Priscilla Rodgers,
M.P.S., NY Lic. Psychoan. Jungian Analyst,
New York City and Millerton, NY

Introduction

Dennis McCarthy

It is this book's premise that life's most pivotal experiences, both good and bad, can only be truly expressed via the language of the imagination. The process of inner exploration, often initiated by these pivotal experiences, is also largely non-verbal at its core. This is especially true for children who do not have the capacity or the need to use words to experience themselves and describe this experience. Children are not yet "in their heads." They live closer to their instincts, their emotions, and their core. Children's natural "language" as such is more multi-dimensional and closer, as a result, to the very heart of life. Consequently it is not a linear language that one can simply learn.

Our intention in these pages is to illustrate, explore, and celebrate the non-verbal and the non-literal experience of children in therapy. The wonderful process of creative transformation that can and often does ensue when therapist and child are playing, whether it be with sand, clay, movement, art, or even spoken language, when used creatively without a simple question-and-answer format, has much to teach us about children and how they best express what has meaning to them. It is the belief of the therapists whose work fills these pages that this non-verbal language is not only the child's primary language but also the only way for them to express and describe their life experiences. The non-verbal allows us to enter a liminal state, one that children live close to, in which things are not static or fixed, and in which great shifts may happen with ease. The non-verbal is in and of itself a means of experiencing a new way of being in one's self, potentially free from the mental concepts that keep us, as adults, stuck, and for this reason also it is deeply therapeutic.

Adults, too, often speak of life's most poignant, disturbing, and exalted moments and experiences via symbols and metaphor rather than in direct language. This approach is less vulnerable to censure, less able to be directed by what we think and more by what we feel. Someone once said that dreams and the body never lie. The images of dreams and the chronic muscular tensions in our bodies are a more direct link to the underlying causes—and also to the thwarted energy that we need in order to be more fully our selves. As a result, an approach to therapy that utilizes dreams, the body, and/or the active imagination in some form will allow us to penetrate our defenses and access the dormant yet positive energies held therein.

Often another person "speaking" in such a manner about their lives can have a healing effect on us, the listener or witness. In David Whyte's poem on page 8, his experience of loss is first expressed via silence, then metaphor, then tears. This sequence is deeply satisfying to witness as well as to experience. We the listeners are moved along the same, age-old human pathway of loss and the seemingly impossible task of integrating this loss into our lives. How do we go on? Even as young children we have many "how do we go on" experiences, both little and big and often unbeknownst to our parents or the world around us. Life itself and the day-to-day process of living it in all its hugeness presents this potential obstacle of how to process and express what is bigger and wilder and deeper than words. Add to this the many personal traumas children are confronted with, and the almost daily collective traumas that all children must somehow reconcile, and the need to speak rather than remain silent is imperative. Yet how *do* we speak about such things?

The therapists included in this book use a variety of non-verbal methods in their work. They encounter a wide variety of unspeakable experiences from a non-verbal perspective, and the children they deal with feel seen and heard and understood as a result. Each of the therapists was chosen for their years of experience in the field and their belief in the power of the non-verbal as it pertains to their own lives as well as those of their patients. For true therapy only happens in the overlap of the child playing and the therapist playing. A willingness to let go of preconceived ideas and to enter the process "feet first", so to speak, is required by both.

Therapy with children today, at least in much of the United States, often consists of asking children to speak in adult language, or speaking to and/or for the child. Even many play therapists use board games that rely on verbalizing rather than letting children be creative. Although the idea that children are small adults has long been dismissed from psychological and educational training, it seems too often to prevail in the therapeutic treatment of children. This may be due in large part to an inability on the part of many therapists to understand the language children speak via play, and to devalue it as a result. It is no longer our language, although it once was.

We, too, once felt that myths were closer to our experience of life. We, too, upon picking up a paintbrush or a piece of clay, felt the immediate satisfaction of knowing that these materials held the potential for self-expression, for the articulation of our entire being, and for the joy of exploring of new ways of self-experience. We knew that we could truly speak with this material, especially if our imaginations were given free reign. And we felt seen by the adult who handed us the paints or expressed interest in our drawings. As small children, we jumped and spun and fell to the ground, laughing out loud—and although we did so for fun, we also did so because we had to. Our spirits spoke via this unbridled movement. All the many disappointments and heartaches, too, were felt rather than thought, experienced physically rather than processed cognitively. We struggled with, and mastered, uprightness and mobility via playful movement and not through verbal instruction. If offered a sandbox and numerous small figures to use in it, we, too, would have felt in setting them up that we were speaking. If we brought the scene therein to life we would have felt some of the same energetic stirrings that leaping and falling elicited and satisfied in us, just by knocking down the worlds we had just created or erupting the sand as if the world was exploding, only to reassemble it all again in our version of Genesis.

It is possible to assess the severity of many childhood problems by the ease with which children utilize creative arts materials: how they draw or move or manipulate clay. The immobilizing effects of trauma can be readily seen in how the child molds clay, moves their body, or encounters a sandbox. Perhaps even more important, it is possible to help the child change simply by helping them better articulate via these materials. It is not so much then what they say via these materials but that they are *able* to say via them.

Perhaps it is the fear of regression to a childish place in ourselves that makes so many adults shun this more primary and ultimately meaningful language. Perhaps we are afraid we will lose control by speaking and listening in a non-intellectual modality. But ultimately we, too, benefit when we enter the labyrinth with the child, wandering in the subterranean darkness there as we seek a way through. We, too, come closer to our collective humanity that lies buried beneath the layers of intellect and limited vision with which we have been taught to view our lives.

Children the world over deal with atrocities every day, and not just the cruelties of the playground or the at times brutal mistakes of our families, but the pains of our fellow humans that children hear about and see each day via the news and the internet, or experience simply by being still psychically connected to the rest of humankind. The horrors of Darfur are not lost on them, as they are many of us. The seeming unwillingness on the part of the adults in power to confront issues such as global warming, out of simple greed, is not lost on the child. In all of the many global conflicts occurring even as I write these words, 80 percent of those killed are women and children. This fact is known by children without reading it in the paper, as they retain vestiges of what could best be called a collective psyche, one which links them to the rest of humanity.

The struggle to reconcile these horrors as each child attempts to navigate, as well, the age-old struggle to grow, cannot be expressed and processed through words. Nor are there any words that we as adults can use to comfort them with, or ourselves for that matter. For us, too, the language of the imagination offers the only possibility of articulating the extremes of life, the hopelessness that we too often feel.

I am struck and touched at how willing most parents I work with are to assume full responsibility for their children's problems. If I were to suggest that these problems came in part from the world around them, they would not like it, precisely because they too feel at a loss to change this world. Their own quick tempers or rigid expectations seem easy to solve in comparison. And yet, no matter how we wish we could protect our children from all of the above, we can only help them to express their response to it and find some way of living and thriving in the shadow of it. For me this can only be done through the imagination, and not as an escapist pathway but as a means of struggling to express the inexpressible.

When a child enters our therapy space, bringing with them the problems or symptoms that have caused the world around them to take notice, we have an opportunity to engage with them in their language, in their world, rather than ask them to speak to us in ours. If we can speak their language, or at least offer it to them as a means of speaking, they will entrust us with not only a willingness for expression that may help us to know what is wrong, but also a means of playing together that will have the potential for real transformation. This can't happen except by using their language, with all its almost magical fluidity that loosens rigidity, strengthens and solidifies weakness, and helps the child's developing ego to continue to do so with grace and integrity.

A very unsocial and seemingly unformed child entered my office last year and refused to look at me, talk to me, or even examine the many objects that I have in my playroom. He knelt by the sand and proceeded to dig. Upon finding some small crystals buried there by another child, he happily exclaimed to me that he had done it. He had discovered them and as a result they belonged to him. He found many more and became happier with each new discovery. He allowed me to hold his treasures and even to advise him the best place to dig. That was all, but that was an important first step. He returned again the following week with an eagerness that surprised his mother. He resumed his digging, continuing to ignore both me and the space, but with a sense of softened musculature, and with a smile on his face. This time his ignoring me felt like the beginnings of a relationship. Allowing him the freedom to be in charge put us in synch with each other. He dug and dug, and when I at one point tentatively introduced a dragon that wanted to vie with him for his treasures, he quickly began to incorporate dragons into his play, pretending at first that I hadn't instigated this, that he had "discovered" them.

Eventually he came to include me in his play, utilize objects from my shelves, and develop the capacity for relating. He did so because I met him where he was: defended against the adult world that had unrealistic expectations of him, and cut off from his peers as well. He seemed, in the words of his teacher, to have no individual identity. But the "I" that emerged as we continued to play together was a very bright and wonderful "I." If I had insisted he speak my adult language, this would not have happened. And as the literal use of language precludes the imagination, there would have been no salvation in it for this child. In his non-verbal digging he had uncovered, and as a result "discovered" himself, with my help and support.

Weeks later, once he had emerged and felt safe and even comfortable enough to be free with himself, he turned to me in the middle of making a sand scene and said, "I really love coming here." This was probably the first actual sentence he had spoken to me, but by the time he uttered it he was already a very different child; social and even outgoing in school, self-possessed and self-confident in his daily life. His words were affirming what had happened, rather than being central to its happening. Much can be said about how and why his simple digging, along with my attentiveness and not interfering, brought about such a significant change. But that it did, and that our common language was that of play, was true.

The act of self-discovery is central to any therapeutic process. This boy's process is an apt metaphor for all creative therapy. By using our imaginations to dig in the material of self, we find the greater Self, or at least resume our lifelong journey towards finding it. We will need to make many changes to accommodate this Self, but playing makes change not only easier, but by its very nature a necessity. All the expressive materials described in this book are non-static, and thus almost all require a letting go of the known form or defense system in order to use them, at least temporarily. Yet all of them also allow for the experience and expression of solidity, without rigidity. This paradox that creative play possesses in all its variants is at the core of its efficacy.

Perhaps the most important aspect of non-verbal work with children is that it satisfies them deeply, helping them to feel seen and heard without losing any of the mystery of life experience. Any attempt to articulate this mystery through simple everyday speech would greatly diminish its power. Ordinary words feel small, whereas life is seemingly limitless. Children welcome this limitlessness. They relinquish their closeness to it slowly and reluctantly—and this in and of itself causes many childhood problems.

A child once told me with a smile on his face and in a hushed voice, as if letting me in on a big secret: "You know, life is a million times bigger than this, a gazillion times bigger!" He had made a scene in the sandbox that was an attempt to display many worlds layered one upon the other. He wanted me to know that the box had limits but his imagination did not. He found great comfort in this, as many children do. We offer this book then, with its canon of techniques and experiences, as an effort to explore the art of speaking about this "gazillion times bigger" world and the child's experience of it.

Chapter 1

The Hidden Treasure of the Self

Jenny Bates

In this chapter I will be exploring the theme of hidden treasure, using my own perceptions, intuitions, and experiences in sandplay with children, and relevant case material. However, I would like to acknowledge the thinkers and writers in the field who have influenced my way of working with children. These include the work and writings of C.G. Jung, D.W. Winnicott and Dora Kalff, and the ongoing inspiration provided by Dennis McCarthy. Last, as a student and practitioner of Shambhala Buddhist teachings, I have confidence in the basic goodness of all beings, beyond conceptual thought or dualistic thinking, and it is from this ground that I work with children as a play therapist.

In my work as a play therapist with children, sandplay is central and essential to the therapeutic process. Using a sandbox deeper than is customary (eight inches deep, as opposed to three or four) has resulted in all kinds of experiences with digging, burying, and seeking treasure. These experiences have aroused in me an interest in better understanding, via my thoughts and observations, the significance of hidden treasure in the world of children who come to play and use the sand.

The beauty of sandplay with children is that the symbol and its place in the sand scene stands for itself, with interpretation rarely needed by, or to, the child concerned. During the course of therapy and the creation of several sand scenes, and as a result of this symbolic play, the child will manifest changes in behaviors in her world that indicate the transformative effects of sandplay and of working in this non-verbal way. Sandplay and the use of symbolic objects that create the scene or story undoubtedly facilitate the integration of unconscious material with consciously held beliefs and feelings. For example, a child is not usually able to verbalize her sense of fragmentation or loss of self-confidence as a result of her experiences or upbringing. The symbol, however, does exactly that. I have come to think that the choice to select, hide, bury, and find treasure is symbolic of a child's sense of self, her emerging "me-ness."

It is as if the child is saying, "My sense of me is valuable, special, and needs to be protected. I can hide it from the world. I will decide how to hide it, who protects it and how, and to whom and when it will be revealed." Thus she gains mastery over a mysterious, organic process of healing and development of identity that is necessary for healthy growth.

When a child is engaged in creating a sand scene of symbolic significance, the therapist serves as a witness and container, sharing in the intensity and unfolding of the creation and expression of something almost sacred, one could say. Sometimes it can feel as though we are standing on hallowed ground.

Case study: Amy

Nine-year-old Amy lived in kinship foster care with her great-aunt and uncle and older cousin. She felt deeply sad about the loss of her father through alcoholism, her mother through mental illness, and her older brother who was living separately. She had been with her foster family for four or five years and was doing well, according to her aunt. Amy had occasional visits with her mother and brother. However, it wasn't long before I heard about the difficulties Amy was having with her older cousin in the home, as well as incidents of petty thieving and the struggle to maintain friendships at school.

I was struck initially by an artificiality in the way Amy presented herself. Her first few sand trays were rich and complicated, verging on the chaotic. They involved all kinds of loss, struggle, conflict, burials, and hidden treasure. After four months of continuous weekly sessions in which Amy established all kinds of physical and imaginative games, in addition to sandplay, she created the following scene:

> First she collected a few items of treasure—shiny beads, glass stones—and put them into a small treasure box, itself decorated with jewels and brass trimming. She buried the box in the center of the sand tray as deep as she could and covered it over with sand. On the surface, over the treasure, she placed a church and next to it a small Christian icon. She then selected other figures of saints and holy people and buried them in a circle around the central church. These were accompanied by church-like buildings. White shells and stones were then half-hidden in a careful arrangement around the central church.

Amy was in awe of what she had created. She had entered a hushed and silent space while creating this scene, had worked with focus and concentration unbroken from start to completion, saying very little. What was remarkable about this scene was its order, its arrangement around a central object. In fact we could call it an emerging mandala pattern, itself a symbol for the Self. Amy's foster family were devout Christians, and it seemed that here she was expressing her growing sense of security in this home, with religion providing a grounding in community and spirituality, both an inner and an outer experience. There was also a sense of laying things to rest. In fact she named this scene "The Holy Graveyard" (Figure 1.1). Amy had recently been taken to the grave of her great-grandmother, after whom she was named. So the symbol here combines Amy's inner self, her lineage, and her present family and community into a pictorial representation. This is something that a nine-year-old would find difficult to articulate verbally.

Amy's therapy process has been the struggle to establish a secure yet authentically felt sense of self. If her immediate family were considered such "bad seeds" by her great-aunt and others in the extended family, what did that make her? She had developed an air of sweetness that was exaggerated simply to protect her from the worst possible threat of all, that is, "Be good, or you will be sent to Social Services," from befalling her. However, in the experiences of choosing, hiding, burying, guarding, and finding treasure over and over again, the artificiality faded and Amy came to stand as truly herself within her foster family. Her inner self now successfully integrates both unconscious and conscious aspects, a process that I believe happens directly in sandplay and specifically in treasure-seeking.

Figure. 1.1 The Holy Graveyard

Sandplay in itself combines elements that are known and unknown. When asked gently why a particular object was chosen, the child most frequently responds with a shrug of the shoulders or possibly "I don't know." The choosing and the placing come from the "I don't know" but the final viewing of the completed scene impacts the conscious mind, often with a "Wow! Did I do that?" type of response. This is all information from which the inner self is constructed. Amy's most recent sand story in this current series involved a treasure chest buried deep in the desert, over which many sandstorms blew. One day a family of tigers came to the treasure site. The baby tiger was chosen to find the treasure, and then the treasure was replaced by an Egyptian mummy that Amy named "T" (short for Tutankhamun). She spoke quietly to T, saying, "You've survived for a long, long time," and then buried him in place of the treasure chest and closed him in. Now that her surviving self is safe and buried, representing a sense of a healthy lineage, her treasure is more readily accessible. She can be herself in her foster family, accepted for whom and what she is. It is healthy to have some aspects of ourselves buried or put away once some light has been shed on them.

Case study: Carla

Carla was an 11-year-old struggling to come to terms with her mother's alcoholism, which had dramatically broken apart her family. Her mother now lived in a separate apartment, while Carla and her younger brother lived with their father in the original family home. One time Carla had called the police when she realized that her mother was driving her and her brother while intoxicated. This had thrust Carla suddenly into a world of adult matters and responsibility. After this, Carla became anxious and hypervigilant about her mother's state and felt a need to take care of her younger brother. I saw Carla for three months in sessions every other week. Carla could talk about how she felt abruptly separated from her carefree childhood, by having to confront her mother's drinking, and how she now felt unsafe around her. She was afraid to be alone at night for fear that her mother would get drunk. Carla was immediately attracted to the sandbox but also delighted in exploring other forms of non-verbal expression, such as messy painting, the doll's house, clay and ball games, all of which served to reduce her anxiety and preoccupation. During the time that her mother gained sobriety in treatment and a measure of reliability, Carla said that she knew she would never be a child again, partly because of what had happened and partly because it really was time for her to be growing up anyway!

Carla herself decided to end sessions when her summer schedule became very demanding, and toward the end of our sessions together she created the following sand scenes in two consecutive sessions.

The first scene Carla named quite early on as "The Artifactual Day" (Figure 1.2). She was recreating a recent school trip to a local archeological site.

> In the sandbox she made several sites, each with differing artifacts chosen from the shelves and marked with a flag. The flags were of differing colors according to a schema that indicated those sites already dug out and those still to be uncovered. The final site was located just off center and was a deep, deep well. Into this she put three treasured articles—a small, heart-shaped clock, a pair of golden slippers, and a small pile of coins. She then closed over the top of the well with a glass tile, a round mirror, and finally a large lotus flower. She marked the site with a large yellow flag. It was different from the others because this site could only be opened by professionals, as opposed to students.

Figure 1.2 The Artifactual Day

Carla was indicating that explorations into her innermost self and secrets (the treasure at the bottom of the well) were entrusted to trained people. This central well with treasure, protected, can now begin to serve as an organizing principle in her life, constructed to contain all of her experiences. Other aspects of herself, represented in the other sites, were more accessible and more available to everyone.

The sand scene in Carla's following and final session was a summation of her life and her family up to this point. Carla was quiet, intent, and focussed throughout the entire, rather short time it took her to put it together. There was a flow in the creating that indicates the accessing of unconscious and semi-conscious material. While this scene does not contain treasure as such, it had a direct connection to the treasure from her previous sand tray. Carla chose six specific items from the shelves and placed them in a diagonal line spaced about a hand width's apart starting from the bottom left-hand corner and moving toward the upper right-hand corner of the box—from unconscious to conscious, one could say (Figure 1.3). She then placed trees and flowers on either side of these six objects to create a pathway. Carla said, "This is a kind of time line." Starting with the first object, she indicated that it showed two people coming together, then the second object the starting of a family, then the nurturing of children, then the growing of children, then the collapse of one of the family members, and finally the heart-shaped clock (a treasure from the previous sand scene). She said this represented her belief that time will heal.

Figure 1.3 The time line

Carla is at the stage developmentally when she can use verbal expression related to the non-verbal process utilized in the sand. Her sense of composure and confidence were palpable to me as she said goodbye. The sandplay had enabled her to put a jarring and challenging experience into a logical, coherent story. She had gained mastery over an unspeakable event and her treasure was now safely back in place. She was now able to spend the night at her mother's home without experiencing her previous anxiety. We all feel more confident when unconscious content has light shed on it and it can become part of our self-expression.

In the world of one younger child, caught up in and confused by the bitter mistrust between separated parents, the treasure in his sandplay was hidden or buried but remained unprotected. It was subject to being found and devoured by a big monster of some kind—a fierce tiger or a raging T-rex or a rapacious crocodile. It felt like nothing was safe in his world, certainly not his precious and vulnerable self. He was not being physically abused in either home, as far as I knew, but his sandplay clearly revealed that he felt unsafe in his situation. There was no safe place for him to be, for his sense of inner security to develop; no protection from the psychological battering. The symbolic play speaks volumes where words are not yet available.

Case study: Veronica

Children use treasure, the symbol of treasure, as a way to speak about themselves, their sense of themselves, their feelings about who they are from the inside. Treasure is an expression of their sense of unique specialness, and how they use it in sandplay gives us a direct glimpse into their psychic world. Veronica, a five-year-old victim of sexual abuse, uses treasure all the time in her sand scenes. Treasure, in the form of hundreds of glass stones, white shells, marbles, and beads, etc., is strewn across the sand tray, in piles, in lines, some buried, some exposed, some in little boxes lying on the surface or buried deep.

This is a picture of psychic fragmentation that is hard to ignore. As she progresses in therapy and her external world becomes safer and more protected, her use of treasure changes and reflects a safer-feeling self. Now the treasure is more contained, more carefully selected, often protected by trees and flowers and surrounded by a fence. Psychically, Veronica is healing. Could it be explained more eloquently?

Case study: Susie

At the other end of the spectrum of treasure play is the work of a nine-year-old girl. Susie is the oldest child of three whose parents were both wishing to find a new way to raise their children together. The father wanted to work part-time from home as a consultant in his business, and the mother wanted to go back to part-time work as a nurse. As a result of their changed financial position they could no longer afford to send Susie to a private school. Susie was finding it really hard to make this adjustment. The local public school not only had very different children but also a very different emphasis on academics. I felt that she had a positive and intact sense of self that was being challenged and had shaken up her relationship to her mother, in particular, with whom she was becoming oppositional and angry at home. In a recent sand scene she did the following:

> She dug a hole to the bottom of the sand tray and cleared a space wide enough to make a mound, on top of which she put a sand-castle. On top of that she put a smaller sandcastle. Then she took a little treasure box with a key to it, put in two jewel-like stones, and placed it on the very top of the tiered castle. Then she dug a hole in the bottom of the mound in which the key was hidden. The sides of the castle were carefully decorated with blue and white shiny stones. Two ladders were placed, available to whomever could find the key and thereby gain access to the treasure, and a white fence

Figure 1.4 Treasure seeking

was put around the castle. Around the four corners of the sandbox she set up flowerpots, each with a specific symbol beside it, and established a kind of treasure hunt with an entry portal and clues along the path, pitfalls and conundrums, a secret bridge, and additional treasure hidden at its base.

Susie was delighted with this creation. Her story felt playful yet challenging, appropriate, and balanced. It was an unfolding journey toward a self that is contained, precious, and available only to the person worthy of it, thus giving us a clear picture of this child's healthy sense of herself in her world. Over the course of her therapy she had navigated a difficult transition from a private to a public school, successfully re-established her place as the eldest child in the family, and skillfully negotiated how to respond to her mother's demands and expectations, while remaining true to her self in her world of books and play. She left the session looking confident and radiant.

In the world of non-purposive play, in an environment that is friendly, safe, and stimulating, children are free to express what they need to express, or feel like expressing, in ways appropriate to their developmental stage. This mostly means finding some form of play that addresses their needs directly without the need to speak about them. Much has been written about the value of play for healthy development, mental, emotional, physical, and psychological. Such non-purposive play naturally comes from the spontaneous, non-verbal aspect of ourselves. As play therapists we respond to the figures, symbols, and scenes created by children as expressions of their inner states of being, much as a psychotherapist responds to the words, dreams, and verbal imaginings of adults.

Play itself is a form of non-verbal expression. The value of sandplay with its myriad of objects, both natural and man-made, is that the child's imagination is freed from contamination by external influences, such as media games and personalities, and can develop in its own genuine way, touching directly on both the inner and outer experience of the child. What is profound about sandplay is that not only does it stimulate expression and transformation but also, through feelings evoked, provides its own interpretation. The completed creation touches the heart of both creator and witness. I have never been asked by a child of any age, "What does this mean?" The meaning is conveyed through the power of the experience and the symbols themselves, letting the unconscious do the work of assimilation and integration as the conscious mind notices and responds to the manifested scene.

My work in this field is an ongoing process of exploration into children's use of treasure as a symbol of self in sandplay. Thus far my observations keep me continuously engaged in this theme that is full of richness and mystery. I hope that these ideas can serve all of us—therapists and children—on our journey toward health and wholeness.

Chapter 2

Getting the Inside Out
Speaking with Clay

Michelle Rhodes

To form something from a lump of clay is to expose what was in the darkness to the light of day, to open up spaces, to invite oneself into the realm of unspeakable memory. In this chapter I invite you to immerse yourself in imaginal clay experience and poetic reverie as I share with you what I have learned using clay to help ordinary, extraordinary children "get the inside out."

Inside-outness is backwardness. Something is not all right. A person may feel inside out when they are out of control, seized by an emotion, or when the boundary between inside and outside breaks down precipitously. To turn oneself inside out, bit by bit, is either self-sacrificial or the ultimate act of faith and trust. "Getting the inside out" can be destructive if it disregards safe boundaries and invades the real space of others, or if it overwhelms and re-traumatizes the patient/artist. These are real dangers when working with clay, and the clay therapist must always be ready to step in to shore up weak psychic structure, and collapsing clay pieces.

Every creation is a destruction of what was status quo before, and this is especially evident when working with a piece of clay. Keeping this in mind, let us consider different ways of working with the clay and how they may function energetically, sensually, kinesthetically, and expressively to bring the inside out.

Forming

The child creates by squeezing, pinching, poking the clay, adding and connecting parts, or cutting away excess to reveal a desired form. All of these techniques may be used by one child, even in the creation of a single work, but it is helpful to understand the special nuances of each way of working. As you read the following descriptions, imagine yourself both as the clay and as the child artist.

Squeezing

You have clay in your hand. You squeeze and it changes shape, conforming to the shape of your hands. Recording the gesture, the clay takes on the shape of the space that was surrounded by your hand. When you look at it you see the shape of what was felt-experienced when you squeezed, translated into an object that now on its own occupies space.

Pinching

Related to squeezing, but performed with fingers only, there is a more peripheral quality to the experience of pinching. The fingers are our upper extremities, far from the gut of the deep inside. Pinching may go so far that it annihilates the substance of the clay, forming windows in what was at first solid but was made so thin as to become non-existent.

Poking

The fingers, together or singly, press into the mass of clay to the center, or through it to the outside.

Squeezing and pinching and poking are the tactile methods, compared with the ones that follow.

Construction / addition of parts

This is a "headier" experience. By that I mean removed from the gut feeling, dissociated from the body experience as a defense against what might be called "uncivilized" wishes and feelings. Construction techniques are more mental than physical. The artist's attention is high, elevated, in the head. The focus remains on the outside of the clay form, emphasizing the boundaries of the clay parts rather than the sensation of the skin experience. The piece is designed rather than developed organically. Children who construct often seek out tools with hard, straight edges, wanting to eliminate any trace of their own hand in the work. Younger children may construct with coils or ropes of rolled clay on a flat surface, as if making a three-dimensional drawing. The flat pictorial effort is related to linear drawing and the forming of letters and writing, a left hand brain task.

Cutting away

Related to the flat construction approach, cutting away can be another effort to bring drawing/writing skills into three dimensions, either through cutting into the thickness of the clay and leaving some parts raised, or by cutting all the way through a flat tile or block with a pointed tool, jigsaw style. Tools are essential to this approach. Traces of the hand are seen as imperfections. Precision is the goal. Intention is valued highly and accidental effects are eschewed.

These are all ways of "getting the inside out" by working with clay, and they are not necessarily reversing the inside and outside, but let us for a moment imagine the body-self turning inside out—a situation in which guts would be spilled, while the protective skin of the self that interfaces with the world would become uselessly trapped on the inside. Gory and gutsy images do emerge when the self opens, but so do soft vulnerabilities, mighty protectors, magical powers, and humor, along with practical problem solving and the experience of mastery. In reading the vignettes, keep in mind the image of an inside-out self, the rawness of the insides, and the various ways in which the children manage their vulnerability.

Vignettes

These little vignettes are not from any one child or adult I have worked with, but rather they are a mix. I hope they convey some of the wordless power of clay work. So, sit back and relax. The curtain is about to go up.

Act I

Scene 1: Poking

> Clay. So lumpy and inert. It sits there heavily. I see the color of the clay—bright rusty red. I need to know if it is something I can use. I reach out and press my index finger into it. How much does it give? How much does it resist? With that simple test of its response-ability (is it something I can trust?) I have gone into it. Just a little poke, but the surface has been broken. I might poke my finger in deeper and wiggle it around in a dark space to discover what is inside. That is a little scary. I can't see what is there. I have made a dark hole. I will get a pointed tool and poke into it. I will get a knife and cut through to it. I will slice it with a string. Now I can see the inside. It seems okay, not scary anymore.

Scene 2: Squeezing

Now I feel safe enough to squeeze some red clay. I grab a handful off the big block and I squeeze it into an irregular, elongated shape, using both hands. The red is on my hands now. I look at my hands, and I am aware of a deep sensation of living flesh and blood and feces. The sensation drops back into wordless sensing and does not take up residence in my conscious mind. It doesn't link up with a psychotic process or a traumatic memory. I can go on. I am not overwhelmed. Nonetheless, the intense iron red of the clay is startling.

I continue squeezing the red clay and folding it and rolling it over and I make it into a ball.

Scene 3: Slamming

I raise the ball up over my head with both hands and slam it down on the table as hard as I can. The loud slapping sound startles me, but is so satisfying. I make it happen again and again, gradually flattening the piece of clay into a thick slab. Looking closely, I see that it has the imprint of the texture of the canvas that covers the table.

Scene 4: Stomping

I drop the clay on a cloth on the floor, lay another cloth over it, and stomp on it. I dance on it, hopping from one foot to the other, until I am breathing hard and my face is flushed. Joyful stomping! I am the destroyer and yet I have killed no one. The bad me, the parts of myself I am ashamed of, I have obliterated. I feel calm.

Scene 5: Reflection

Carefully I peel away the cloth, soiled from my stomping, and set the delicate slab of clay on the table. I notice the imprints of the bottoms of my shoes. It makes me smile. My body is still tingling from the hopping dance as I consider what I shall make with this clay. I decide to leave it just as it is, except I add my initials, writing with a pointed stick. Later I will glaze it and take it home. Here is something I have put my stomp-stamp on. I have really made an impression. I want to impress my mother. I can't wait to show her this gift of my true self. Will her face light up, or will she scowl and look confused?

Scene 6: Checking

I am working fast. I don't bother with realistic details. I grab bits of clay and stick them here and there and draw on it with a stick. I mark some areas with poke holes and crosshatching to show danger and hiding places. In less than a minute I am done. I can't wait to show my mother. I run to the door to see if she is here yet. I do this several times. Then I have to use the bathroom. I hear my mother at the door, and tear out of the bathroom, forgetting to zip up my pants.

Act II

Scene 1: Scooping out

I sit at the table with a lump of sandy, pale gray clay and a sturdy loop tool. One scoop at a time I dig in and remove a curl of clay about the size of a melon ball. It could easily fit in my mouth. I think this but I don't put the clay in my mouth. I continue taking "bites" out of the lump with the loop tool, until there is only a pile of "bites" and a hollowed out shape. I save both the bites and the bowl, but the bowl has holes already, so I make more holes and then the bowl falls apart. Somewhere in me is aroused a recognition that the "bites" are unspeakably filthy and the bowl is scraped out so completely it no longer exists. I feel my insides scraped empty. I feel weightless, hollow, and sad, but I can tolerate sitting with this feeling, because the clay is in front of me.

Scene 2: Transforming

Now in my mind I see the breakfast table. I am having a bad memory. A cereal bowl. Some milk accidentally spilled. I squeeze what was the bowl and the bits of scooped out clay into a lump and make a witch with bulging eyes and a gaping toothy mouth. I need some red iron oxide paint to make blood running down her jaw. The rusty red paint appears before me and I am grateful but unquestioning. I feel the presence of a protective, facilitating figure, but I don't think about that or turn around. I am thinking about my mother and I am focussed on the sculpture I am making. I imagine my mother watching me. I wonder if this toothy mouth would scare her. I make the blood. I take a pinch of gray clay that turns pinkish from the red iron oxide on my hands and I make a tiny helpless figure half hanging out of the monster's mouth.

Act III

Scene 1: Dissolving

Some thin, sandy, gray clay slabs have gone "bone dry" and I don't want to keep them. I wrap them in a cloth and hit it with a wooden mallet. I unwrap the pieces and drop them one by one into a basin of water, where they make sizzling sounds as they sink, absorb the water, and gradually disintegrate into mush. They were weak and fragile. There was no way to fix them. Dissolving them is a satisfying solution.

Scene 2: Storing away

I pour off the water from the dissolved clay and stir the soft clay slurry. I put it in a jar. I can use this sandy soft mud to mend and bond clay pieces I will make in the future. What was weak and fragile becomes stuff for toughening up and holding together.

Scene 3: Constructing

I decide to make miniature bricks. When I build a wall with them I use the sandy, soft mud for the mortar. It looks so real! Bricks and mortar: red clay for the bricks and sandy gray mush for the mortar. I feel like a real builder, constructing this wall brick by brick, bonding the bricks with my mortar.

Act IV

Scene 1: Quiet boy

I observe the boy from a little distance but I cannot tell for sure what he is making. It looks like someone in a dentist's chair. I think that perhaps the boy has been traumatized by a dentist or some other large person looming over him, inflicting pain while he lies helpless. I ask him, when he is done, what he has made. He tells me it is a person strapped into a rocket ship, about to go off into outer space.

Scene 2: Monster-maker

I am an experienced clay artist, formerly the quiet boy. I enter the space confidently, ready to work. As I have done every week for the more than two years I have been coming here, I create a monster, skillfully and with great care for detail. I explain its toxicity, magical powers, and great size. I make up another part of the continuing saga of epic battles and alien super-monsters. In my head I see flames shoot from its eyes. It devours whole cities with its snarling maw, determined to capture the magic jewel hidden somewhere in the heart of the city. That jewel is my own creativity and I am capturing it, but I don't know that yet.

Scene 3: Inside/outside encounter

I am creating a scene in the sand, using several monsters I have made out of clay. Some I have made out of a mixture of clay, sand, paper pulp, and glue. Now they are solid and dry. They feel substantial and especially durable and resilient. If I want, I can add to them at any time. I sense their earthiness when I handle them. They have weight and presence. Great battles ensue. There is a sturdy brick wall as part of my sand scene. Some army men hide behind the brick wall but one of my monsters knocks the brick wall over and gets through to them.

Act V

Scene 1: Boobs

Boobs, boobs, and more boobs. With the other ten-year-old girls, I come to terms with my changing body, sculpting naked women with generous breasts. (It's all right to do that here.) The clay is the earth mother herself. We look at pictures of ancient goddesses and invent our own.

Scene 2: Asshole

I am feeling mischievous. Well, actually I feel squirmy. I make an asshole, then I don't know what to do with it. The other girls giggle and scowl, rejecting me. I want to make a penis, but I don't. I look gleeful, but inside I feel so sad. I am glad when the clay lady puts my piece away on the shelf. She says it's all right to make anything, so I guess it is. Then I make a ballerina. I wish I could be a beautiful ballerina. I wish I could talk to my mom every day and snuggle on her lap. I wish she could come and see me dance in ballet class, and then I would run into her arms and she would hug me and tell me I am her wonderful, beautiful girl.

Scene 3: Owls

I make a tree full of owls. It's a big family: mother owl, and five or six baby owls. I hope they'll be ok. They might be too much for the one mother owl. Sometimes I feel like I'm more than one girl.

Act VI

Scene 1: The wheel

Sitting at the potter's wheel, in the silent space that touches me, I hold steady, steady, steady, learning where my center is from inside, using breath, observing the response of the clay as it spins in its own stillness or wobbles off center.

Scene 2: Centering

Feeling the clay lady's steadiness and strength supporting me, I can hold steady. I discover my own strength and steadiness. I experience this as solely my own. In this moment, the stillness, the strength, and the steadiness are mine. I don't know where I'm going in life. I see my dreams shattering and falling all around me. It's hard to remain hopeful. This working on the wheel helps me feel more in control. We can begin to imagine a future. Each rotation of the wheel holds me and binds me to the world, keeps my center inside. Then I can begin to process my feelings with words and make a space inside for wisdom's tiny seed to take root. I can come to terms with the seriousness of my situation, and not spin out of control.

On clay and regression

When I tell people that I use clay for art therapy, they often comment that it must be a direct route to regression, particularly angry, messing regression, because clay is, after all, so much like feces, and so how wonderful to have permission to play with it. My response is that perhaps all creative endeavors in any medium or modality invite regression to infantile behaviors. I would argue that historically the most culturally primitive clay experiences seem to have been more about reproductive functions, and that the smearing of feces that occurs in madness and infants is more of an act-hunger being satisfied: smearing things feels good, whether it's feces (if one is an infant and as yet uncivilized, or mad), or puréed carrots and peas or mud or chocolate icing, or expensive artist's oil paint; smearing gushy stuff is basically pleasurable. It stimulates the skin of the hand with a sensation of smoothness, wetness, and temperature. Even manipulated by a brush, experiencing its give may remind us of early tactile pleasures. It doesn't resist us.

In a primitive, completely regressed state, squishing experiences are one way to sense our boundaries, to define ourselves spatially, to know inside from outside. Before an infant has experienced squishing something with his fingers, he has experienced the squishy feeling of feces passing from his body, and that is associated with the pleasure of relieving the inner pressure of the approaching bowel movement. I am thinking twice now about the infant's hands and what they have touched, and I am wondering if inside the womb the mature fetus feels the contact squishiness with his entire body, and I wonder what of that squishy contact experience is remembered by the body after birth—is some of that memory aroused when we touch something squishy?

Alchemy

Clay passes through many states, of course, though we usually think of it as soft and malleable. It has hard and dry states, as well as raw and cooked. It can even melt and boil. It can be crushed to powder, dissolved. It can settle and separate out its finer and coarser particles. One speaks of a clay "body," which is made up of substances with different qualities, resulting in something appropriate to a particular use and process. There is brick clay fired hard, and clay mixed with straw and sand for house building. There is elegant and refined porcelain clay, and even clay for healing, cleansing, or decorating the human body. Each state of clay is a possible metaphor for a psychological experience, and this is the basis for considering clay work as alchemical.

Material / metaphorical states of clay

Clamber down a riverbank with me, and we'll find it there, washed clean of earth, stuck in some tree roots, in heavy, slippery chunks. It may be red, ochre, pale gray, white, or charcoal black. In it are stones and sand, perhaps even some detritus of human manufacture. To begin with we will let it dry, to a stage potters call "bone dry." That means all water will have evaporated, leaving the hunk of clay hard and bleached looking. It has lightened and now incorporates air instead of water. What would it mean for a psyche to "dry out" and become "light," "porous," and "brittle"? It might have required a lot of grieving. For a child, that might mean a lot of "bad" or angry behavior. A safe place must be made for the child to be "bad" and witnessed, and accepted, even loved, for the badness. Let us imagine then that the child has had a good number of such sessions, and is now "dry."

In this state the hunk of clay is fragile and ready for change. It is at this stage most easily broken into small lumps and sprinkled into a tub of water, where it instantly begins to dissolve. The bits of dry clay become a layer of soft mud covered with clear water. They have become formless but not chaotic. Clay is down and water is up. The clay mass at this stage contains discernibly different elements, some finer, some denser, some of different colors. I can pour off the extra water and stir the mass of mud vigorously, integrating all that parts into a new whole. Something has been lost, the definable residues of former shapes. All are actually present, though now in integrated form, each adding useful and interesting qualities. We could have gone another route, though, incorporating the finer elements and removing the un-dissolved larger particles. We could have subjected the mass to magnets to remove iron particles. We could have mixed it with an excess of water into a thin liquid, and let it settle. The more water, the finer the separation of elements, the more they can be seen and studied. Decisions must be made about the parts that have been separated out: shall it be discarded or saved? Stored and filed away for future coloring and texturing, or ground to a powder with mortar and pestle?

Case study

A case example comes to mind from work with a child whose mother had gone off to have a life, seeing her daughter a few times a year, for holidays. She would not know the intimate details of her daughter's maturation through her school years and adolescence. The sadness in the girl's heart over this abandonment was like a stone in the clay, and other feelings were like some pockets of sand, bits of dark peaty substance, and some veins of red iron oxide. I worked with the girl on separation issues by engaging her in a drying, dissolving, and separating process with "wild" natural clays dug outside the studio, and different colors of clays from unwanted sculptures. We broke up the dry clay, filled a vat with water, and dropped the clay bits in. After that she lost interest. I decided to work on it side by side with her while she did her own clay sculpture. As I worked she became interested and curious. Then I explained to her what I was doing, and asked if she wanted to try some separating along with me. This introduced separation as an experience of differentiation and allowed her to work through her feelings of loss, one pebble or grain of sand at a time.

After the clay has been mixed or separated, it can be dried on an absorbent surface such as plaster or porous bricks. Then it can be kneaded and reused to make new sculptures or vessels. That is when we could mix some of the separated materials back in. Psychologically, such elements may represent rejected memories, wishes, or feelings that the child was too immature or emotionally raw or shattered to take in. There needed to be a refinement, a simplification, before they could be reintroduced. To do such a process with a child is to communicate an understanding of the child's losses, fragility, grief, strengths, and needs. The child needs to put the pain aside for a while and build up her own sense of goodness and self. Then she can begin to integrate the temporarily removed bits. They may have sharp edges. She can be in control of introducing such elements into the clay, discarding them, or saving them for another day.

Case study: five-year group

A group of three boys was formed gradually and met for several years to do expressive clay work with the option of learning the basics of the potter's wheel. They were given no assignments and the few rules there were existed solely to encourage the boys' freedom of expression.

Figure 2.1 Fiery red serpent with gold spikes, by Charles

Charles

Charles began with individual clay sessions. He was seven years old, almost eight, and very talkative, with the vocabulary of a much older child. He knew exactly what he wanted to do and initially accepted no instruction. Whatever stresses there might have been at home, he rarely spoke of them. By contrast he often spoke about his numerous small pets: spiders, snakes, lizards, beetles, and so forth. He observed the world in great detail and perceived in four dimensions: three, plus time/movement. When Charles made clay sculptures of creatures, they were twisting and turning, spreading their wings, moving in all directions in space. They were constructed with an awareness of bones, joints, and muscle. Their stories included whole ecosystems: how and what they ate, what habitat they required, and (of great importance) how they captured and subdued prey and defended themselves against enemies (Figures 2.1, 2.2). Charles' parents supported his interest in animal life in many ways, his father through his knowledge of biology, and his mother by a keen interest and enthusiasm for wherever Charles' curiosity led. She had nurtured his creative mind with storytelling and explorations of the natural world in their own back yard. Charles was wiry and like quicksilver. He was almost always chewing gum, which seemed to help safely disperse the energy which otherwise tended to tumble out of his mouth in little "tskk" sounds, like the sound of a drop of water hitting a hot iron. In his creative enthusiasm, paint and clay would spread like wild fire. His shop apron, quickly and carelessly tied, gave the impression of flying in the wind and falling off him at every turn. The ties would come undone and drag on the floor. He would take no notice.

Figure 2.2 Creature with cone spikes, by Charles

Alex

Alex joined Charles after several months. A year older than Charles, Alex used few words to express himself and was receptive to instruction that he followed carefully. Alex rarely initiated. Completing one step of a project, he would not forge ahead to the next phase. If no instruction was given, he might sit in a dreamy state. Awakened from his reverie, he was always cheerful and ready to do his next assignment. His sense of humor was subtle and just below the surface, ready to break through (Figure 2.3). Alex was athletic but thin and his clothing hung loose on his frame. This clothing was usually a soccer, basketball, or softball uniform, as Alex was active in all those sports and was generally on his way to or from a game when he came to the studio. Alex's enthusiasm for competitive sports was somewhat dampened by his intense seasonal allergies, for which he was often medicated. I suspect the combination of allergy and medication was at least partially responsible for his tendency to drift off. Precise and careful in his execution of tasks, Alex did not make messes, which was a good thing, because he often forgot to put on his shop apron. He said one day that he hated art class in school, especially when he was told to "just be creative," because at such times his mind would go blank. He developed his own way of creating figures that were solid and funny and sometimes weird, but rarely toothy, which set them apart from the creatures the other boys made.

Figure 2.3 Shark skier, by Alex

Oliver

The following year, Oliver, about Alex's age, joined the group, and this trio was to stay together until the group disbanded. Upon entering the group, Oliver announced that he was a cartoonist. He always carried a sketchbook and drawing materials. An only child, and the only boy of the three who had traveled abroad and frequented art museums, Oliver brought a touch of cultural sophistication to the group. Oliver was more interested in indoor activities than the other boys, and didn't particularly enjoy exerting himself physically. He was a user of tools and was not eager to get his hands dirty, although he did sometimes handle the clay directly, as in this demon's head with bloody teeth (Figure 2.4).

Figure 2.4 Bloody-toothed demon, by Oliver

Oliver was above all a planner and a draftsman, and at a remove from the physical world. His first work was a relief of one of his cartoon characters (Figure 2.5), and he maintained this interest in two-dimensional clay projects until the end, by which time he was creating richly colored and elaborately detailed painted surfaces (Figure 2.6).

Collaboration

Early on the boys shared a common fascination with fantasy monsters. Charles and Oliver continued with this theme, developing and refining their projects over the years, trading ideas, co-creating. By the end, they were truly collaborating, planning creatures together, each contributing what he was best at. Alex also participated, although his contribution was most likely to be an offhand remark playing off a suggestion made by one of the others. He was part of the animated planning and discussion of the creatures, their physical traits, magical powers, color of details. Meanwhile, he would be doing his own thing, something more related to everyday experience, but complicated and challenging technically, and sometimes with a humorous twist, like the shark skier. Oliver became the expert at surface detail, painting and mixing colors, while Charles provided biologically based details (Figure 2.7).

Figure 2.5 Cartoon character, by Oliver

Figure 2.6 Gilded monster, by Oliver (detail)

In the course of the years that the group met, Alex suffered some serious losses. A beloved aunt died of cancer, and one winter night the following year his house, the home he had lived in all his young life, burned to the ground. By that time he had made many clay sculptures and some fine bowls. All but one piece were destroyed (Figure 2.8). Fortunately, no one was hurt,

Figure 2.7 Blue snake with red and gold detail, by Oliver and Charles

and soon Alex returned to the group and set out to create a new body of work. From time to time, he would share some of what had happened. The sense of support in the room became palpable at such times, as the boys became quiet, and then ventured a few consoling words.

The trio looked forward to their time together, even as they balanced on the cusp of adolescence and it became nearly impossible to fit the group time into the demands of their various schedules. Still they clung to their old interests as long as they could, making more refined and elegant and potent creatures than ever before, until finally they were really done with it. In the end, it was Charles who would have kept coming, had the other boys stayed with it, but he wouldn't come on his own. It was the mutuality, the shared creativity that had become so special. Alex had found his artistic side and exercised his esthetic sense, Charles had developed as a team player, and Oliver had begun to break free of rectilinear space and explore muscularity. The experience of working together with clay had helped each to become a little more whole, accepting, vulnerably strong, and sensitive to the nuances and subtleties of being an authentic individual within a group.

In preparing this chapter for publication, I interviewed the boys about their experience in the group. I was struck by the affection all three boys expressed toward their artworks and their memories of shared creative time. As Charles put it, "We fueled each other's imaginations, and it just spiraled up. We never could have thought those things up on our own." Oliver said,

"We were all equal, no one was the leader, and that's what was so nice about it." Alex has a special attachment to the one clay piece (Figure 2.8) that survived when his house burned down. When I visited his new home to interview him, I held the precious figure in my hands, its formerly blue-green glaze still blackened with the residue of the inferno it survived.

Figure 2.8 Alien, by Alex

Acknowledgements

Special thanks to all the children whose creative work showed me ways of working with clay that I would never have imagined. All the authors listed below have informed the way I think about what I do. Shawn McNiff and Mary Caroline Richards have touched my life personally by offering much needed encouragement, and to them I will always be especially indebted. And Dennis, our editor: without your vision this chapter, waiting for too long to be written, would never have happened. Thank you.

Further reading

Ackerman, D. (1990) *A Natural History of the Senses*. New York, NY: Random House.

Bachelard, G. (1964) *The Poetics of Space*. New York, NY: Grossman Publishers.

Blatner, H.A. (1973) *Acting In: Practical Applications of Psychodramatic Methods*. New York, NY: Springer Publishing Company.

Edinger, E.F. (1985) *Anatomy of the Psyche: Alchemical Symbolism in Psychotherapy.* La Salle, IL: Open Court Publishing Company.

Henley, D. (2002) *Clayworks in Art Therapy: Plying the Sacred Circle.* London: Jessica Kingsley Publishers.

Hillman, J. (1983) *Healing Fiction.* Barrytown, NY: Station Hill Press.

McNiff, S. (1992) *Art as Medicine: Creating a Therapy of the Imagination.* Boston, MA and London: Shambala Press.

Montagu, A. (1971) *Touching: The Human Significance of the Skin.* New York, NY: Harper and Rowe.

Moore, T. (2004) *Dark Nights of the Soul.* New York, NY: HarperCollins Publishers.

Richards, M.C. (1962) *Centering: In Pottery, Poetry, and the Person.* Middletown, CT: Wesleyan University Press.

Sherwood, P. (2004) *The Healing Art of Clay Therapy.* Camberwell: Australian Council for Educational Research.

Wiener, D.J. (ed.) (2002) *Beyond Talk Therapy: Using Movement and Expressive Techniques in Clinical Practice.* Washington, DC: American Psychological Association.

Chapter 3

Speaking with the Body
Using Dance/Movement Therapy to Enhance Communication and Healing with Young Children

Claire LeMessurier and Susan Loman

Before children have words, they communicate non-verbally. The body stores pre-verbal memories that offer a way to understand early childhood dysfunction and trauma. This chapter will present how dance/movement therapy (DMT) techniques can be used to help children build attachment, increase self-regulation, express unspoken feelings, re-work unresolved developmental issues, and heal from trauma and loss. Case studies will illustrate how dance/movement therapy approaches provide children the opportunity to get in touch with their bodies and speak through movement in a healing process that helps children become integrated and whole. A theoretical framework will be presented that combines a developmental and relational approach through the modality of dance/movement therapy.

Dance/movement therapists use dance and movement to connect with clients, help them explore social and emotional dynamics, express feelings, build self-regulation, and integrate the whole self. Using an approach that combines relational, and developmental perspectives, dance/movement therapists use the body and movement to help caregivers and children work through challenging behavioral issues. Movement is used for assessment, to build therapeutic relationships and as a way to support clients in healing.

This powerful, ancient, creative mode of healing helps young children tap an instinctual core self to re-work problem areas non-verbally and build new pathways for healthy development. Movement interactions teach relationship skills and self-regulation. Early trauma memories held in the body can be processed and healed through this medium, speaking a language that is readily available for all ages.

Movement is the primary mode of communication for young children. The same is true for adults, where studies show that between 50 and 90 percent of communication occurs on a non-verbal level; when words and body expression contradict each other, however, we believe the non-verbal message. Very young children, on the other hand, rely on non-verbal information for most of the communication in their relationships with others, since they are only just beginning to learn how to use words.

Children use movement to tell us how they feel and what they need. Relationships and emotions are demonstrated through the body: muscle tension, facial expressions, body shaping, eye contact, breath, gestures, and full body movement. Dance/movement therapists observe the movement qualities in children and caregivers very carefully and use their own bodies to try on the client's movement and to attune with the person on a body-felt level. Children are very responsive to this; most very young children seem to engage quickly in relationships when they see others connecting with them non-verbally. The technique of attunement, or reflecting muscle tension, rhythm, or body shape, can be quite effective for developing non-verbal empathy.

Movement therapy with young children can be done individually, with families and in groups, always keeping in mind a family-centered approach that is child-focused. Claire LeMessurier works out of a rural community mental health center in an impoverished area. Young children, ages birth through six, have a range of emotional, behavioral, and developmental concerns, often related to a mismatch or clash in the parent–child relationship. Generational poverty, substance abuse, domestic violence, and child abuse often result in attachment problems and issues of complex trauma.

Mental health services provided for young children are grounded in developmental knowledge, understanding that in early growth there are many phases where children go through a disorganized period as they attain a new level of maturity (Kestenberg 1975; Kestenberg Amighi *et al.* 1999). The overall approach was relationship-based, based on the premise that we grow through relationships and that as therapists we relate to clients in such a way as to help them find what they need to heal (Jordan *et al.* 1991). Services were supportive and respectful of the family system and were infused into existing early childhood networks and responsive to the community needs.

Dance/movement therapy approaches

We (the authors) approach dance/movement therapy sessions with children with the belief that clients themselves know what they need to heal (Brooke 2006). There is an expectation that children, given the opportunity, will communicate what is important to them and, if given attention and support, will play/move out their stories to find a solution and integrate growth on the whole person level (Bromfield 1994; Levy 1995).

Young children use movement and play modalities to reveal themselves and "work" on issues through body expression. The dance/movement therapist focuses on being fully present with the child, showing an openness and anticipation for the unknown that becomes an invitation for the child to be authentic. The therapist follows the child's lead and acts as a facilitator in the healing process.

Somatic attunement is used as a primary tool in the therapeutic relationship to build attachment and show body-felt empathy (Harvey 1994; Loman 2005; Sandel, Chaiklin and Lohn 1993; Tortora 2006): dance/movement therapists attune to clients using their own bodies by trying on movement qualities seen in others. Duplicating the tension flow quality can validate feelings and show kinesthetic empathy (Kestenberg 1985; Loman 1994, 1998). Reflecting a body shape can build on trust in the relationship (Eberhard-Kaechele 2007; Loman and Foley 1996; Loman and Merman 1996). Attunement is done in various ways, depending on the developmental stage of the child, the stage of therapeutic relationship, and the particular work. Very young children usually enjoy "complete attunement" (Kestenberg 1975), but older children (between the ages of four and five) might not want this intense level of exact attunement. They may reject it as mimicking, unless they are working on early developmental themes that require close matching.

An ongoing goal is to support progression through developmental phases and healthy growth (Loman 1998). An environment may be created to help a child explore movement dynamics that encourage joyful play and growth. A key concept is to provide creative outlets for expression of developmental and emotional release (Loman 1994)—for example, a baby is given a scarf to play peek-a-boo and explore object permanency; a soft ball is used to practice give-and-take engagement; an angry child is given playdough to pound or a large therapy ball to kick or a balloon to hit. The therapist encourages the child to enhance and expand its range of movement to provide greater options for self-expression and problem solving.

Building self-regulation is an important task of early development that grows out of a caregiving relationship (Sossin 1999, 2007; Stern 1985). Similar to a parent or caregiver, the dance/movement therapist matches the movement quality of a child and then either enhances or reduces the quality to teach self-regulation. By means of help to modify negative states and amplify positive states through non-verbal interactions, children learn to regulate themselves and experience good feelings.

Validating emotions, increasing feeling recognition, and learning to identify feelings are goals to support young children's social and emotional development. Understanding feelings and being able to read non-verbal expression are important for successful social interactions (Kornblum 2002).

Discharging negative emotional content physically helps us think clearly and prevents physical illness (Goodill 2005). Children seem spontaneously to find physical outlets for their feeling expression—sometimes in ways that are not acceptable (Kornblum 2002). Dance/movement therapists can help children channel aggressive feelings into safe expression to release negative impulses.

Caregiver–child relationships and attachment

Parents and other caregivers are extremely important influences in young children's lives. Whenever possible, we want to include them in the process of therapy, as we consider them as experts on their children and able to make the biggest difference in promoting attachment and positive relationships (Loughlin 1999; Meekums 1991).

Problems sometimes occur in the parent–child relationship for a variety of reasons, such as illness in the parent or child, the child's special needs, mismatching temperaments, divorce, and teen pregnancy, to name a few. Partnering with parents to understand and support children with special needs, the dance/movement therapist helps them attune to their children through psycho-education, role modeling, movement, and play and observes the movement dialogue between parent and child, looking for times of matching rhythms and affective sharing, to find ways to build on these emerging skills. Noticing when clashing rhythms occur in the relationship is also vital in order to find ways to bring awareness of the differences and to work on mutually satisfying patterns. We also educate parents and caregivers to support and hold their children to promote trust and security. Parents may also need support for themselves in exploring how their own experience of childhood can affect their parenting.

Case study: failure to thrive

Annalee, an eleven-month-old child, was diagnosed with failure to thrive. She had not been gaining weight and was in an area of concern for growth, according to the pediatrician. She held her body in a rigid posture while her watchful eyes followed her mother in a hypervigilant manner. She was only just learning how to crawl. Regarding feeding, she drank from a bottle that was propped up for her, often spit up formula and had not yet been introduced to solid foods. When her mother moved quickly, Annalee flinched, turning her head abruptly away. Her young mother had a history of abandonment, physical and sexual abuse, and an eating disorder. Her first child lived mostly elsewhere.

The dance/movement therapist started the therapy with a home visit to begin to build a relationship with the mother, hear her concerns, and observe the parent–child relationship. She reflected the mother's movement qualities in her own body to acknowledge the level of the mother's concern, while Annalee lay in a car seat on the floor. The therapist observed that the mother mostly remained at a distance from her baby, who also seemed content to have some distance. Annalee did not smile or play spontaneously, but remained ever cautious. She responded very little to the dance/movement therapist's efforts to interact with her.

After a period of assessment, the dance/movement therapist decided to work with the mother to improve the feeding relationship. Mother was encouraged to feed Annalee solid food in a high chair. At first the mother was resistant, complaining that baby did not like it. After a level of trust was built, the mother allowed a feeding time to be videotaped, to receive feedback about the feeding relationship and to work on plans for remediation.

While watching the video with the mother, the approach was to focus on when the feeding worked well. A movement clash between mother and child soon became evident, but luckily there were moments of success. In the video, the mother moved with a fast, abrupt quality that was very focused. Annalee seemed slow to react, moving very gradually with an indirect approach to the space around her as she looked around to find the spoon. The mother would immediately move the spoon to Annalee's mouth, but give up before Annalee moved her head and mouth to the spoon. The mother quickly became frustrated and gave up, usually withdrawing the spoon before Annalee coordinated her mouth to open it. As the mother became more relaxed, her feeding arm slowed down enough (and maybe Annalee sped up) so that Annalee got a mouthful. The mother was able to see these movement dynamics and correct her feeding style, with the result that Annalee gained weight.

Exploring the deeper aspects underneath the movement clash was more difficult. The dance/movement therapist worked to create a therapeutic alliance with the mother, trying to support and hold her in a way that she might do for her infant. The dance/movement therapist directly modeled caregiving that was attentive and nurturing. She supported the mother in trying on Annalee's quality of movement and becoming more present with her baby.

Discussion

Understanding that children have their own movement styles and preferences educates us in how to approach children individually. Working with this mother on attunement exercises helped her to get to know her child's temperament and further the process of mother–child bonding. A great variety of feeling tones is conveyed through tension changes evident in facial expressions and body motions. For example, peacefulness is recognized by even or gradual tension changes, while excitement may be expressed through high intensity and abruptness (Kestenberg Amighi *et al.* 1999). These individual tension-flow patterns can be used to improve understanding of potential areas of harmony and conflict between family members, and to assist them in understanding each other's feelings.

Feeding and attachment difficulties surface when there is a lack of attunement between child and caregiver, as we have seen in the case of Annalee and her mother. Learning how to provide secure holding for nursing or bottle-feeding, to soothe a crying baby, and attune to a baby's needs can be extremely challenging. The dance/movement therapist can offer valuable techniques, such as matching the child's muscle tension and using breathing rhythms to create a feeling of dynamic support. This approach encourages the use of similar intensity in the voice and movement to convey the feeling that the caregiver is fully present. Caregivers learn how to create mutuality and attunement that leads to empathy, while meeting the infant's needs for nourishment, support, soothing, and secure attachment (Loman and Adams 2005).

Complex trauma

The term "complex trauma" refers to exposure to multiple traumatic events such as child abuse, neglect, and witnessing domestic violence or war, that may have immediate and/or long-term impact on children. Complex trauma often interferes with the development of a secure parent–child relationship, which affects the development of self-regulation and interpersonal relations. Complex trauma in young children can affect multiple domains including attachment, brain development, affect and behavioral regulation, dissociation, and self-concept (Cook *et al.* 2007).

The National Child Trauma Network recommends six core components for treatment: establishing safety; improving self-regulation; building self-reflective skills; integrating traumatic experiences; practicing relational engagement; enhancing positive affect (Cook *et al.* 2007). The therapist partners with the parent or caregiver to support the child in growing in all these domains, and may recommend individual, family, or group therapy.

Trauma memories are held in the body and may be healed through the body. Dance/movement therapists use movement and play to support young children who are experiencing complex trauma by addressing the domains listed above in an integrated fashion. Included in the therapeutic process are the developments of a secure holding environment, attunement to children on a body level, and following the child's lead in play and creative expression, while supporting self-regulation. Children are guided to explore and expand on themes, label experiences, and develop life narratives. The authors believe that children experiencing complex trauma who have the opportunity to build long-term therapeutic relationships may be able to work through more specific abuse details through movement re-enactment and use of a healing re-choreography (Lewis 1993). This in-depth work often takes place during the second year of treatment.

Case study: Erika—long-term individual dance/movement therapy for early re-parenting and sexual abuse issues

Erika was referred to treatment at the age of two, due to early neglect and abuse, which occurred while she was living with her biological mother. Additional concerns were that Erika was not gaining weight and her hair was falling out. She recently had moved in with her father and stepmother, who experienced extreme poverty. Although these parents were very upset about Erika's previous abuse, they too were often very harsh in their treatment of her. Her stepmother put her to bed as a punishment and screamed at Erika if she moved. At meal times, Erika had to eat at a small table away from the adults and finish everything before getting up. This could take hours and did not promote weight gain. The stepmother had a history of trauma and eating disorder and had a large body and an expansive, intrusive and controlling manner.

Erika was small and made herself even smaller by contracting her body shape, keeping it still with rigid tension. She appeared hypervigilant and looked around with darting eyes (see Perry et al. 1995). She was often observed wringing her hands. On a few occasions, her eyes and face expressed her interest in being playful. She asked the dance/movement therapist if she could hold the baby doll and wrap it carefully in a scarf. If she spoke baby talk, even in play, her parents reprimanded her.

Initial goals in therapy were to partner with the parents and help them reflect on their children's needs. The first six months were spent doing home visiting, listening to and empathizing with the parents' concerns, nurturing the family by helping them get their practical needs met, and working to strengthen the parent–child relationship. It became apparent that Erika needed therapy sessions outside of the home to have a safe place to heal.

Dance/movement therapy sessions were set up to be consistent and regular, to encourage trust. The therapist would pick up Erika at preschool each week and walk a block with her to the clinic. The walk together was a part of the therapeutic interaction where trust and attachment issues were often explored.

Themes for the first six months of individual therapy centered on building trust, role-playing mommy and baby, creating boundaries and safety around touch, managing anxiety, and expressing anger. Every session, Erika requested "to do playdough." Often this would occur when Erika felt angry during the session. She would knead, poke, punch, press, and cut the playdough to express her feelings, while the therapist attuned to her movements. Erika would frequently create a bedtime scene and ask the therapist to sit near her as she pretended to sleep, sometimes asking to be held.

Due to the unfortunate circumstance of the father's illness, therapy was interrupted for about five months. When dance/movement therapy resumed, Erika began to work on a deeper level to heal from her early abusive experiences. Following her lead, the dance/movement therapist supported Erika in reparative developmental work. She began regressing in therapy to work on early nurturing and feeding issues. Since Erika had wanted to suck on doll bottles, the therapist got her a real baby bottle to use only during dance/movement therapy sessions. Consistent rituals were created for filling the bottle with water and later washing it out after the play and putting it away in a regular special place. The ritual included giving Erika time to de-role and come back to her older self before leaving the session. For six weeks, Erika repeated her sucking ritual, often sucking peacefully on her bottle for 10–15 minutes, with the dance/movement therapist sitting close by and attuning to her sucking rhythm through sound and movement.

In one session Erika became more directive as she set up a bedtime scene: "I want this blanket on me, then the giant puppy, then that other blanket. Now you sit over there and be the mother watching TV." There was a feeling of distance. She sucked on her bottle and pretended to go to sleep; then abruptly in the dark she let out the screeching yell of a very distressed baby.

In a later session, she insisted on having a carrot. She said, "You need to feed me. Feed me that carrot!" She enjoyed biting with much strength to break off a piece of the thick carrot, and crunched it in her mouth with great satisfaction. "More," she said, asking to be fed more. She repeated the biting and chewing over and over. The dance/movement therapist sat close to her, attuning to the new biting rhythm that had tapping quality. Erika shifted in this session from the indulgent quality of sucking to the fighting quality of biting, which helped her move from a symbiotic, uniting phase to one promoting separation. She appeared to be re-working early issues related to feeding, nurturing, and attachment.

In the next session Erika set up another bedtime scene. "You need to feed me now. I am hungry. Feed me the apple pieces. No, put them in my mouth. I am a baby!" The dance/movement therapist calmly fed her small bites of apple, one by one. Erika enjoyed biting them and was not satisfied until the whole apple was gone. She seemed to be continuing to explore this stage of initial separation, re-working issues related to feeding, infant care, and abuse.

In the next session, Erika said, "Make a high chair for you to feed me in!" This time she sat up in a chair, and leaned forward, asking to be fed apple pieces. She held her body like an older child. After this feeding, she spied colorful ribbon sticks and wanted to dance. With harp music of her choice playing, Erika gave half the ribbons to the therapist and began to dance. She smiled and indicated non-verbally that she wanted the therapist to mirror her movements exactly. After much joyful dancing together, she drew a picture of a girl with a dress on, dancing. Erika now seemed happier. She had played out a more mature developmental stage and enjoyed expressing herself through dance and being closely mirrored through movement. This progression of sessions demonstrated a re-choreography of early attachment issues (Lewis 1993) re-enacted through the ritual of feeding.

Discussion

When the dance/movement therapist began to attune to Erika's emotional expression through shared body rhythms, she provided the basis for bonding and attachment.

The Kestenberg Movement Profile (KMP) is a complex instrument for describing, assessing, and interpreting non-verbal behaviour (Kestenberg *et al.* 1999). The KMP is movement-based and employs a movement vocabulary. For dance/movement therapists who use movement as a language and a medium for diagnosis, treatment planning, intervention, and interaction, the KMP is an excellent tool. The KMP bridges non-verbal behaviour with psychological theory and interpretation. It outlines an individual's level of developmental functioning, movement preferences, areas of psychological harmony and conflict, and relational development.

The first stage of development in the KMP framework is the sucking rhythm (Kestenberg Amighi *et al.* 1999). While nursing or feeding the baby a bottle, caregivers and therapists can connect to the baby through sharing the sucking rhythm. Matching the muscle tension changes through humming creates a feeling of mutuality and trust (Kestenberg and Buelte 1977). The dance/movement therapist was able to enter Erika's world by creating movements and sounds that matched Erika's rhythm. A harmonious connection was then created.

As Erika regressed and went through this first movement stage in a satisfactory way, she was then able to evolve into the next phase, the biting stage. The dance/movement therapist recognized the developmental progression and was able to adjust and adapt to the new rhythm as it emerged. Children are continuously evolving and growing, and having knowledge of the developmental progression of the KMP is a helpful guidepost for therapists in identifying where the child is developmentally.

Case study: Bruce—attachment and aggression

Bruce was initially referred to treatment just prior to his third birthday, after being excluded from eight different daycare settings for aggressive behavior. His young and single father, who struggled with significant mental illness, cared for him. Bruce's mother had left when he was one year old, and he suffered neglect, confinement, and witnessed inappropriate adult behavior. A very active child, Bruce frequently rushed towards objects, crashing into them and then abruptly changing focus. He seemed extremely hyperactive, moving frantically in and out of rooms. He offered very little eye contact, did not respond to nurturing, and sought relationships only to meet basic needs. His father provided little structure and tended to be in his own world, sometimes delusional and often on the computer. Mental health services initially focussed on building parenting skills and supporting Bruce in being successful in a preschool setting, while also helping the family assess what services they needed.

Bruce's life became more safe and consistent when he was placed in a therapeutic preschool setting with a one-on-one aide, and after his father was connected to mental health services. When Bruce was four-and-a-half years old, he was placed in individual dance/movement therapy in order to build attachment and to provide him with a contained holding environment to express feelings and practice self-regulation. Weekly dance/movement therapy sessions complemented other services by giving Bruce a place to do deep emotional healing work, at the same time as learning how to function socially in the classroom.

Bruce began the school year aggressively pushing peers out of his way, behaving in hurtful ways towards other children. After a period of individual work, Bruce gradually contained his aggression, began to interact with peers a bit, and was able to participate with other children in groups.

Bruce seemed to understand the process of therapy naturally. The dance/movement therapist set clear, simple guidelines for safety and maintained strict boundaries around time, touch, and cleaning up. These guidelines helped Bruce relax and feel safe and begin to connect in relationship to the therapist and address very difficult complex trauma and attachment issues from his early life. The small therapy room seemed to help contain the sometimes frightening work.

The dance/movement therapist followed Bruce's lead and attuned to him, to his large and fast movement when he was upset. She would also mirror his full shape and then make a smaller shape, using a less intense dynamic to help him diminish his expression, self-regulate, and begin to calm himself.

Bruce would often veer back and forth between expressing feelings in a more contained way (pressing, punching, and poking playdough), and then expressing them fully (pressing his whole body against the pillows, punching them, and jumping on them).

Over time he began to tolerate longer moments of connection with the dance/movement therapist and to want more attunement. He initiated playing peek-a-boo with scarves. Bruce also became more trustworthy and demonstrated that he could walk to the session next to the therapist without holding hands.

As the therapeutic relationship developed, Bruce was able to explore deeper areas of trauma. Themes in therapy shifted to an earlier, non-verbal developmental stage, with much rage directed towards the mother figure. Bruce found a cylindrical container that he could just barely fit in. "Close me in so I can't get out." He squeezed himself into the can, first rolling around with delight, then pretending to be stuck and becoming very angry. He repeated this movement play for several weeks, always breaking free at the end. It seemed to represent a time when he had been unable to move freely and had possibly been kept contained or bound for extended periods of time (as in a car seat restraint). By being in control of the play and replaying a traumatic experience in his own way, Bruce was able to master his anxiety, express anger safely, and begin to heal.

After a while, the play evolved into a different scenario of containment. "Wrap me up in the big scarf!" Bruce directed. He lay curled on the floor, eagerly anticipating being wrapped, seeming to like the close touch. "Now you open me up!" In what seemed to be a birthing game (Tortora 1994), replayed over and over in the next weeks, Bruce became a special gift that was discovered and joyfully welcomed into the world. He also reversed the roles and wrapped up the dance/movement therapist, "discovering" her with joy. During this time, Bruce became more organized in his play and gained more self-control at school.

Discussion

Some of the highlights of the dance/movement therapy approach used with Bruce were: creating and maintaining a consistent "holding environment" (Winnicott 1965) that established a basic trusting relationship; channeling aggressive impulses into appropriate and interesting motor avenues; and strengthening the child's movement resources so that he was better able to cope with challenges in the environment.

The feeling of safety and trust was fostered through the "holding environment" that was created by providing a space for Bruce to explore his surroundings fully. The children's space was "child-proofed" so that there were no objects that Bruce could hurt himself on. The safe environment increased Bruce's comfort, responsiveness, and involvement. The consistent presence of the therapist was extremely important for Bruce as they became more and more comfortable with each other. The structure of the session was very consistent and stable. The room was always arranged the same way, so that Bruce could predict what the environment would look like and where he could find treasured objects. Predictability in relationships provides the safety for trust to flourish and for creativity, spontaneity, and feelings to be contained.

Props such as scarves, parachutes, soft balls, hoops, and stretch material are considered "neutral" objects. Children can use these materials in their own individual way to help them express their moods and feelings. For example, if a child comes to the session in an angry mood, a scarf can be waved vigorously up and down, or thrown, which helps the child creatively express these feelings. If, on a different day, the child were sad, the scarf could be waved slowly and delicately. The therapist can reflect these expressive movements with another scarf and begin to create a theme that promotes mutual understanding. Sharing movement communicates support and recognition and builds a sense of self-confidence in children. At other times, a scarf may become a bridge between people. In Bruce's case, the scarf was used to help him play through a birthing experience.

Conclusion

Early childhood is a time when essential aspects of development occur, in a way that affects the lifespan. When problems emerge due to communication failures, lack of self-regulation, trauma, or other behavioral issues, early interventions can positively influence future growth. The therapeutic modalities of movement and dance build on children's innate ability to engage in the non-verbal realm and use the body as a medium for attunement, expression, and healing. Young children need to be encouraged to stay present in their bodies in order to integrate social, emotional, physical, and spiritual aspects of self in their development. Dance/ movement therapists use their own bodies as a tool in therapeutic relationships to reflect body-felt empathy and encourage client growth.

A developmental dance/movement therapy approach provides the foundation for understanding the underlying motor qualities in children's growth. Non-verbal methods are used for soothing and to promote healthy attachment. Through the understanding of a predictable developmental sequence, caregivers can learn to empathize with their children and build healthy communication patterns. They can follow the child's lead and redirect aggressive behaviors into satisfying and creative outlets.

References

Bromfield, R. (1994) *Playing For Real.* New York, NY: Dutton.

Brooke, S.L. (2006) *Creative Arts Therapies Manual: A Guide to the History, Theoretical Approaches, Assessment, and Work with Special Populations of Art, Play, Dance, Music, Drama, and Poetry Therapies.* Springfield, IL: Charles C. Thomas.

Cook, A., Spinazzola, J., Ford, J., Lanktree, C. *et al.* (2007) 'Complex trauma in children and adolescents.' *Focal Point 21,* 1, 4–8.

Eberhard-Kaechele, M. (2007) 'The regulation of interpersonal relationships by means of shape-flow: a psycho-educational intervention for traumatized individuals.' In S. Koch and S. Bender (eds) *Movement Analysis: The Legacy of Laban, Bartenieff, Lamb and Kestenberg* (pp.203–211). Berlin: Logos Verlag.

Goodill, S. (2005) *An Introduction to Medical Dance/Movement Therapy: Health Care in Motion.* Philadelphia, PA: Jessica Kingsley Publishers.

Harvey, S. (1994) 'Dynamic play therapy: an integrated expressive arts approach to the family treatment of infants and toddlers.' *ZERO TO THREE Bulletin of National Center for Clinical Infant Programs 15*, 1, 11–17.

Jordan, J.V., Kaplan, A.G., Miller, J.B., Stiver, I.P. and Surrey, J.L. (1991) *Women's Growth in Connection: Writings from the Stone Center.* New York, NY: Guilford Press.

Kestenberg Amighi, J., Loman, S., Lewis, P. and Sossin, M. (1999) *The Meaning of Movement: Developmental and Clinical Perspectives of the Kestenberg Movement Profile.* New York, NY: Brunner-Routledge Publishers.

Kestenberg, J.S. (1975) *Children and Parents.* New York, NY: Jason Aronson Inc.

Kestenberg, J.S. (1985) 'The flow of empathy and trust between mother and child.' In E.J. Anthony and G.H. Pollack (eds) *Parental Influence: In Health and Disease.* Boston, MA: Little, Brown and Co.

Kestenberg, J.S. and Buelte, A. (1977) 'Prevention, infant therapy and the treatment of adults, 2. Mutual holding and holding oneself up.' *International Journal of Psychoanalytic Psychotherapy 6*, 369–396.

Kornblum, R. (2002) *Disarming the Playground: Violence Prevention through Movement and Pro-social Skills.* Oklahoma City, OK: Wood and Barnes.

Lewis, P. (1993) *Creative Transformation: The Healing Power of the Arts.* Wilmette, IL: Chiron Publishing.

Levy, F. (1995) *Dance and Other Expressive Art Therapies.* New York, NY: Routledge Publications.

Loman, S. (1994) 'Attuning to the fetus and the young child: approaches from dance/movement therapy.' *ZERO TO THREE Bulletin of National Center for Clinical Infant Programs. 15*, 1, 20–26.

Loman, S. (1995) 'The case of Warren: a KMP approach to autism.' In F. Levy (ed.) *Dance and Other Expressive Art Therapies.* (pp. 213–223). New York, NY: Routledge Publications.

Loman, S. (1998) 'Employing a developmental model of movement patterns in dance/movement therapy with young children and their families.' *American Journal of Dance Therapy 20*, 2, 101–115.

Loman, S. (2005) 'Chapter 4: Dance/Movement Therapy.' In C. Malchiodi (ed.) *Expressive Therapies* (pp. 68–89). New York, NY: Guilford Press.

Loman, S. and Adams, M. (2005) 'The KMP in action: application of KMP concepts in a community setting.' *Conference Proceedings: 40th Annual Conference of the American Dance Therapy Association.* Columbia, MD: American Dance Therapy Association.

Loman, S. and Foley, F. (1996) 'Models for understanding the nonverbal process in relationships.' *The Arts in Psychotherapy 23*, 4, 341–350.

Loman, S. and Merman, H. (1996) 'The KMP: a tool for dance/movement therapy.' *American Journal of Dance Therapy 18*, 1, 29–52.

Loughlin, E. (1999) 'The shared dance: dance therapy with mothers and infants in the hospital outpatient infant clinic.' *Dance Therapy Association of Australia: Dance Therapy Collections 2*, 37–42.

Meekums, B. (1991) 'Dance/movement therapy with mothers and young children at risk of abuse.' *The Arts in Psychotherapy 18, 3, Special Issue: The creative arts therapies and the family*, 223–230.

Perry, B., Pollard, R., Blakley, T., Baker, W. and Vigilante, D. (1995) 'Childhood trauma, the neurobiology of adaptation, and "use-dependent" development of the brain: how "states" become "traits."' *Infant Mental Health Journal 16*, 4, 271–291.

Sandel, S., Chaiklin, S. and Lohn, A. (1993) *Foundations of Dance/Movement Therapy: The Life and Work of Marian Chace.* Columbia, MD: Marian Chace Memorial Fund of the American Dance Therapy Association.

Sossin, M. (1999) 'Chapter 10: The KMP and Infant-Parent Psychotherapy.' In Kestenberg Amighi, J., Loman, S., Sossin, M. and Lewis, P. (eds) *The Meaning of Movement* (pp.191–209). New York, NY: Brunner-Routledge Publishers.

Sossin, M . (2007) 'History and future of the Kestenberg Movement Profile.' In S. Koch and S. Bender (eds) *Movement Analysis: The Legacy of Laban, Bartenieff, Lamb and Kestenberg* (pp.103–118). Berlin: Logos Verlag.

Stern, D. (1985) *The Interpersonal World of the Infant.* New York, NY: Basic Books.

Tortora, S. (1994) 'Join my dance: the unique movement style of each infant and toddler can invite communication, expression and intervention.' *ZERO TO THREE Bulletin of National Center for Clinical Infant Programs 15,* 1, 1–11.

Tortora, S. (2006) *The Dancing Dialogue: Using the Communicative Power of Movement with Young Children.* Baltimore, MD: Brooks Publishing.

Winnicott, D.W. (1965) *The Maturational Process and the Facilitating Environment.* New York, NY: International Universities Press.

Chapter 4

Speaking with Silence
Play Therapy with Selective Mute Children

Brenda Lawrence

Silence can be a powerful and compelling stance, a way to control one's environment; particularly useful, if in certain circumstances, the possibility or pressure for verbalization engenders fear and anxiety so profound as to strike one mute. This chapter will explore play therapy as the treatment of choice for the childhood condition known as elective or selective mutism.

The author will share case material on several successfully treated young children aged five to seven, from her practice over the course of the last twelve years, in which play therapy choices such as sandplay and puppetry, combined with bioenergetic outlets for aggression, such as battacas (foam bats used for play fighting), pounding clay, jumping, and leaping, were always spiced with humor and accompanied by laughter. The results have been effective and curative.

In Denmark there is an ancient legend of a blind and elderly king whose kingdom was in grave danger from a warring and destructive faction. The despondent king threatened to fight the enemy himself rather than passively allow the loss of his kingdom's freedom. A young man spoke up, offering to fight the impending battle. This man spoke confidently and with apparent insight and wisdom concerning the current situation. When he had finished speaking, the king asked to whom the unfamiliar voice belonged—and was told that it was, in fact, his own son. The king was in disbelief for, as everyone knew, his son had been born mute, and his name, Uffe hin Spage, actually meant "meek, submissive, and quiet." The son revealed that, up until that day, he had been content to let his father do the talking, but now it was necessary for him to defend his country. The king was incredulous, but in time the true nature and strength of his son became evident, for Uffe saved their land and freedom. (1500-year-old Danish tale)

What forces, within or without, could render someone who has the ability to speak, mute? Exposure to violence or other traumatic events can do that, but there are numerous children and adolescents, who have not been subjected to trauma, who struggle with a complex anxiety disorder known as selective mutism. They often speak normally in settings such as home, where they feel comfortable and secure—but even then only to certain persons. Most speak to both parents (but not always), to their siblings, and a few others in their world of family and friends. This way of being is seldom seen as a problem, until the child starts formal education and is not able to participate verbally. In a social situation such as school, where there's an expectation for speech, these children become speechless and uncommunicative. Their fear can be so extreme that a physiological response is triggered, the outward signs of which are the well known symptoms of panic, increased heart and respiratory rate, sweaty palms, lack of facial expression, and rigid body stance. Uninformed persons often misconstrue the child's silence as willful or stubborn behavior.

Selective mutism has apparently been with us since ancient times and there are numerous theories about its causes and possible treatments. My writing on this subject will not be in a scientific manner or through an in-depth review of the literature, but primarily through my direct experience of working with a number of select mute children and their families.

Some current thinking in the field points to a genetic predisposition to developing selective mutism, with a possible link to a small, almond-shaped area of the brain, the amygdala. The amygdala is believed to be instrumental in receiving signals of potential danger from the sympathetic nervous system, and in turn sets off a series of signals in the service of self-preservation. This phenomenon of "fight or flight" becomes an autonomous response to perceived dangers, which, for select mute children, are certain social situations. This neurologically focused investigation validates what I have intuited for years as I have observed the painful fear and panic, dread, and avoidance that these children experience. In addition, all the families with whom I've worked who have a select mute child contain histories of extreme shyness and/or anxiety disorders. In fact, detailed histories of such youngsters often reveal signs from infancy of anxiety discomforts such as separation anxiety, sleep disturbances, inflexibility or rigidity, extreme tantrums and moodiness, as well as severe shyness. All of the parents with whom I've worked identified between two-and-a-half and three years of age as the beginning of their child's problems. Cases of selective mutism in bilingual families add further dimension to issues around speech and communication.

Another area of current research involves the premise that serotonin pathways may be involved in the mediation of the anxious, obsessive qualities of both selective mutism and its close cousin, social phobia. In the last 15 years psychopharmacology has been an increasingly popular treatment choice for selective mutism, and there are numerous case studies in which the commonly prescribed medications are selective serotonin re-uptake inhibitors or the older heterocyclic-type antidepressants.

Today, one can more readily find books and articles on selective mutism with a wide variety of treatment choices: psychopharmacology, psychotherapy, behavioral therapy using a combination of positive reinforcement and desensitization, cognitive behavioral therapy (which focuses on helping the child redirect their anxious worries and fears into positive thoughts), family therapy, art therapy, and other expressive art therapies, including play therapy. I use what I know best and heartily believe in: the efficacy of play therapy. Little, however, has been written about play therapy and other expressive modalities as treatment choices for selective mutism.

Early diagnosis and treatment is best, as this condition is extremely painful for the child and family and really holds the child back from fully participating socially, emotionally, academically, and from just being wholly themselves. These children, over time, develop methods to get their needs met that don't require verbalization. Often others will speak for them and the mutism is reinforced. It becomes much harder to reverse such ingrained patterns. By not speaking in those tense situations, anxiety may decrease with habituation to the persons and the place, but at such a high price in vital energy thwarted. Selective mute children are very often little dynamos, with so much to say and do, and often yearn to be more participatory. Being scared to death hurts. One person described their childhood experience of being a select mute as having to "always be on stage with dreadful stage-fright."

My method of helping these children is quite simple. The goal is to make them comfortable and relaxed by lowering their anxiety through play and laughter. Sparking their creativity and imagination in the free and protective space of the playroom is the beginning, and over time the therapeutic relationship itself becomes part of the cure. For the first few weeks of therapy I see the child twice a week and have a parent, sibling, or friend, someone with whom the child is comfortable and already converses, to be part of the play sessions. My belief is that once I'm invited into the child's world of persons with whom he or she can speak, I can then become a bridge between the child and family and the larger world outside the home. The child's speech begins to open up once the taboo of speaking outside of the select few is broken. They can usually still be described as shy, but are not paralyzed by anxiety that keeps them from more fully participating in life.

Pressuring these children for speech does not work. They shut down. But once they're engaged in the play process, their silence speaks volumes. Providing the unconditional forum for play and expressiveness allows these children gradually to let down their defences and begin to open, to create, and let their imaginations blossom. The silence is frequently broken with laughter. Some children will make animal or motor sounds right away, and sometimes they just forget to be silent and speech bursts out. Having so much fun playing while feeling free and secure enough to do so is an antidote to anxiety, and usually within a few sessions the mute child begins speaking in my presence.

My tools are the sandbox and miniatures, puppets, dolls, and other toys. In addition, art supplies for painting and drawing and clay for sculpting are on hand, as are outlets for aggression—monster drawing, foam bats for battles, clay for pounding and smashing, a small trampoline and giant pillows as safe havens for leaping. Recording devices, toy telephones, and a karaoke machine have, in some instances, stimulated the urge to communicate.

Case study: Sam, aged six

From day one Sam loved the sandbox and the pretend kitchen. In his second session he fed sand with a tiny spoon into a hollow dinosaur until it could hold no more. He would then empty it and begin again, over and over. It felt to me like a hypnotic, but seemingly soothing, ritual. Then he moved on to the play kitchen, pulling out pots and pans and placing them on the little stove.

I'm an instigator at times and had already set the precedent for a big, red lobster to bite me—and sure enough the lobster started nibbling my fingers, which made Sam giggle. Spontaneously I shouted, "This lobster can't make me scream!" and I taped up my mouth, which really caught Sam's attention. Watching me closely, he began feeding himself the pretend food he'd just cooked. I was hopping around, grunting and pointing to my taped mouth while he, with relish, was eating the "food" and licking the spoon. I kept dramatically acting out my frustration. I felt I had traded places with

Sam: without words I was saying, "Look at me! This is you!" I could sense that he wanted so badly to talk.

Sam yearned for more time with his father, who lived about an hour away. Fortunately, his father agreed to come to one play session a week. This involvement made things move quickly. As his father was talking to me and Sam about an upcoming class trip the two of them were going on, I could clearly see that Sam wanted to tell his dad something, so I pushed my chair away from them a bit and said "Go ahead, Sam, I'll just cover my ears," and for the first time they conversed in my presence. Sam's voice was low and soft. A line was crossed.

Next time his father was present I asked Sam to draw himself as a monster, any kind of monster he'd like to be, and he drew a small dinosaur with a long neck.

Figure 4.1 Monster drawing by Sam

I introduced a user-friendly little tape recorder and showed them how to use it, then asked Sam to record any scary sounds his monster could make. I let them know I'd be on the other side of the room with my hands over my ears. It worked like a charm. Sam would growl into the recorder, his father would call me over, and they'd play back the monster's sounds. I'd scream and cringe from the "terrifying" roars. We did this four or five times and

Sam got louder and bolder, to the point that I joked from across the room that it wasn't working for me to cover my ears. By the end of the session Sam was speaking in my presence—not spontaneous speech, but replying to his father's questions.

In the next few sessions Sam used two toy telephones I had set out. I'd make a ringing sound, and he'd pick up the phone. At first he spoke so softly I couldn't hear what he was saying, so I asked him to talk louder as there was too much static on the line, and he did. Within a few sessions he no longer needed this device and began to speak spontaneously. Gradually he began speaking in the classroom and in the after-school program he attended.

When Sam became comfortably verbal, he could be more accurately tested and was found to have several developmental and academic delays that could then be addressed. Sadly, once Sam could talk at school, his father became, once again, an absent, under-involved parent.

Case study: Sarah, aged five

Sarah's first school experience was a half-day kindergarten program in a small elementary public school. Some days of the school week, my office was just across the hall. In November, Sarah's teacher came to me puzzled and upset. In all her years of teaching she had never had a child who was completely uncommunicative, shy, and withdrawn after so many weeks of school. Sarah had not yet become comfortable with the other children, nor had she uttered a single word. As a rule children were immediately drawn to this teacher, who was a warm but firm educator, well liked and respected by all. History-taking revealed a child who fit the profile for selective mutism.

Sarah's mother joined us for sessions in the first few weeks of therapy and shared with me her daughter's belief that her kindergarten teacher just didn't like her. Sarah was supersensitive to voice modulation, and this big-boned teacher had a loud voice at times, which from Sarah's perspective meant the teacher was angry and yelling at her. So our sessions began.

Sarah wasn't comfortable with sand on her hands or on the toys, and used the tabletop to create very detailed, action-filled scenes, primarily with figures from her favorite movie and book, *Pocahontas*. I was genuinely very interested in her play and showed it, laughing or looking sad, emoting what appeared to me appropriate to the unfolding drama Sarah created. She diligently and silently acted out what took place. When someone spoke, the mouth of the figure would be held up to the listener's ear, or when an angry person attacked someone, the figure would fly across the room. Her mother confided to me that this kind of expressive, imaginative play was a new style of behavior. Sarah's mother became a staunch ally in the play therapy process in which her daughter became immersed. Sarah began whispering more details of the story of Pocahontas into her mother's ear, then her mother would intentionally make mistakes in the story, which made her daughter so frustrated that she'd forget to whisper and just spoke out loud what was really "right." Within four sessions Sarah was speaking spontaneously in my presence. This quickly carried over into the classroom and enlarged the extended circle of persons to whom she could comfortably speak.

Sarah had skipped the "terrible twos" and was a very good little mother's helper. She seemed to view being loud or assertive, or anything akin to aggression, as "bad." In very expressive monster drawings and powerful battles with the battacas, the dynamo within Sarah found a forum. In fact, she told me that her first monster "eats people, screams, throws things, breathes fire, and has lots of power."

Figure 4.2 Sarah's first monster drawing

When she became more comfortable with the sand, she began creating almost weekly an evolving hospital scenario on the tabletop, and a big swimming pool in the sandbox where people and sometimes animals would "drown" or go "under." Drowning didn't mean dying, for helpers (at first the eldest sibling, the mother, or doctors and nurses) would rescue those going "under." These scenes were created slowly and carefully, with a highly charged intensity.

In one session, which seemed a turning point in Sarah's process, the father went "under." A female child tried to rescue him, but had to enlist the help of the mother, a doctor, and then another doctor, who finally rescued the father and took him to the hospital (on the tabletop). The injured father was outfitted with multiple bandages for his head, arms, and legs. From that point on a change occurred in Sarah's play. Instead of someone from the pool scene taking the hurt person or animal to the hospital on the table, the doctors and nurses began coming to the pool and would transport the victim or victims to the hospital for assistance.

After that scene Sarah, as many children do after a particularly intense play time, took a two-week break from working in the sand and played with what I call "lighter" materials.

The next time Sarah worked in the sand, she seemed to pick up right where she left off, placing the heavily bandaged father by the side of the pool with the rest of the family. No one was taken to the hospital that day, but the mother and a doctor saved a girl who went "under," and the doctor pulled out several children who had disappeared beneath the water. At the end of the session, Sarah carefully cleaned the sand off each person and placed them beside the father, who was still standing by the side of the pool. As Sarah found her voice and her inner power, the two scenes—the hospital on the tabletop and the pool in the sandbox—had merged to just the one in the sand.

Four months into treatment, Sarah created a very different scene. The sand tray became a castle with a road on the left side of the box. Three knights guarded the entrance to the castle. The interior of the castle was represented by a wide trench or hollowed-out area in the middle, that ran the length of the sandbox. The king was seated on his throne at the far end. Three men on horseback came to visit the king. After a while the horses and their riders, as well as the king, lay down and went to sleep. Quietly, a mother and daughter attempted to visit the king, but left when they realized he was fast asleep.

Eventually, everyone woke up and the king was visited by a large group of people, almost filling the box. The visitors were seated along three of the castle walls, with the king on his throne forming the fourth side of the rectangular shape. Most of the guests departed, except for one family: a mother, father, daughter, and son. The daughter rode away on a horse and returned bearing gifts for the king: a mother pig and several piglets. Next the son left on horseback and returned with a lion as a gift for the king. He rode off again and appeared to be gone a very long time as his sister became agitated, peering down the road repeatedly and showing signs of distress. At last the brother returned with a camel for the king. The children embraced. There was a numinous quality and an emotional, spiritual intensity to this unfolding tale, that made me think of the "adoration of the magi."

Our play sessions began in November and by the end of the school year in June Sarah could no longer be described as a selective mute child, for her frozen tongue was a thing of the past. During one of our final sessions I asked her what she thought was the saddest thing that could happen to a person and she answered, "When somebody can't talk. That happened to me."

Sarah is now a senior in high school and aspires to be a writer.

Case study: Beth, aged five

Figure 4.3 Beth and her dog drawn in the first session

Beth had many fears and perfectionistic tendencies. Her mother and sometimes her older brother were part of the early sessions, and speaking to me came rather quickly. Frequently a family of monsters, a mother, father, and baby, were our playmates. We taught them to jump on the trampoline and to dive into mountains of big pillows. I remember Beth jumping on the little trampoline, holding her mother's hand, as we sang the alphabet song and counted to twenty in an effort to teach the baby monster his lessons. The little monster turned out to be an apt student, then suddenly turned into a real terror, biting, spitting out his vitamins, and on and on.

In the last session before I left for my first vacation since beginning our work together, the baby trashed the playroom, but with care not to break anything. The shelves and everything in the room were emptied onto the floor. Beth made sure her mother saw just how "bad" the baby had been, and with wide eyes her mom kept to the context of the play, remarking on what a mess the baby had created. Beth's demeanor in the world outside home was normally shy and fearful, whereas in the comfortable ambiance of home her behaviors were more akin to the baby's, as she could stamp her feet and slam the door at will. Now her ability to be herself, no matter what the setting, was increasing.

In the sandbox Beth's first creations appeared to be chaos, wherein vast quantities of every kind of miniature filled the sandbox.

Figure 4.4 Early sand scene by Beth

As this play became more organized she used all the miniatures of dogs and cats, usually portrayed as strays in evolving tales of the animals' adoption by various members of a family—a mother and father and two children (just as in Beth's real-life family).

Next came weeks of flooding the box, making lots of mud, swamps, and sinking sand; then began the mud wars. Beth would saturate the sand with water and direct me to mound up the sand into two very high mountains with a deep ravine in between. We'd then choose—or rather, she would choose—the creatures that would be on our separate teams, and the battles would begin. My characters never had a chance to do anything but be totally defeated. Her warriors could cheat or do whatever it took to win, then they'd celebrate, basking in the glory of victory! This time of playful control by a child who was not yet "in control" of her world, particularly the world of school, was vital to her growth.

Outside the therapy room it was spring and then summer. In the garden pond Beth and I caught and released countless frogs. She was a masterful frog snatcher and became self-confident and happy, relaxed and vocal in that role.

Once Beth's anxiety had been reduced and her speech unblocked, she made and verbalized to us her decision not to speak at school until the beginning of the new school year. She said that it would be "too weird" to start speaking in the classroom and to the teacher when she'd gone all year being silent. True to her word, from the first day of the new school year she talked at school and has not stopped since.

Case study: Alysson, aged eight

Alysson and I were only able to work together during her fourth year at school, when she was eight. She had never been identified as having a problem, and consequently had not received any help at all during her first three years of school. She had never spoken to anyone in the school setting, except for a female friend of her own age who was also in her girl scout troop. Neither of Alysson's parents could attend sessions, so her friend joined us for the first few weeks.

Alysson seldom worked in the sand, preferring to play with the dolls and pretend food, and to draw herself as a monster. In fact, it was her recurring monster, "Baby," who helped Alysson to begin to unblock her speech.

Figure 4.5 One of Alysson's Baby Monster drawings

We created stories together about Baby, eventually getting Baby to record "silly" sounds into a tape recorder.

Once Alysson was comfortable recording sounds I announced one day that it was "time to teach Baby to talk." That day I had brought in a baby book with one word and its picture on each page. Alysson and her friend made their own version of the book with illustrations of the words they wanted to use. We took turns. Each girl would record her words while I was out in the hall with the other child. Then we played for Baby each of the girls' recorded words, and that day Baby learned to use words, not just sounds.

This use of the tape recorder became Alysson's way to bring some speech into school. We went to the library at her school and to the one in her neighborhood, and chose books to record. She was a good reader and proud of her reading skills.

After reading together and recording numerous books at school and at her home, I asked Alysson if she'd like to play some of her book recordings to a child in her classroom, to the entire class or to her teacher. Alysson chose to share these with her teacher. She could have chosen none of those possibilities, but I was happy that she didn't take that option. Eventually, she didn't need to use the device of the recorder, and would read directly to her teacher. We started a reading group during lunchtime every school day, and each week Alysson would choose another person to join the group. It became a social boost for Alysson, as classmates would come to her and ask to be part of the lunchtime reading group.

That year there were two other girls in third grade who were not select mutes, but were painfully shy and avoided verbalizing as much as possible. I started a group called "Fun at School" for those three girls, and we just played and laughed together for eight weeks. We created sand scenes, paintings and drawings, jumped rope, made up games, and created puppet shows. We spoke and sang through a karaoke machine, which made their overly soft voices dramatically loud. The monsters they created had a ball with that machine, making their deafening howls and growls. All three girls became comfortable speaking spontaneously to each other and me, and became more confident at school and in the community.

Alysson's treatment for selective mutism was incomplete, as that was the only school year I was able to work with her. She had made some progress, but was not able to participate fully in the world of school and the community. I've been told that she continued to speak softly to teachers and some peers and would read upon request at any time to anyone.

Case study: Jennifer, aged five

For the past few years I have lived and worked in the Caribbean, and once again have had the opportunity to work with children with selective mutism. Jennifer did not speak at all until she was three, and speaks with a severe speech impediment. Her ethnic heritage is both African and Spanish, with both English and Spanish spoken at home and by the extended family on her mother's side. I have never seen a child display such rigid body language. For several sessions Jennifer was robotic, her body held stiffly, with arms pinned tightly to her sides. She made no eye contact and made no facial expression, even with her mother present.

Her imagination and intelligence are quite phenomenal. She adored the puppets and made her first sounds in the playroom with a cow, and then a big wolf with fangs that liked to bite and taunt me.

Jennifer's sand creations were at first made in complete silence, except for some whispering in her mother's ear. She created in the sand slowly, thoughtfully, and with much detail. One scene had an airport with a runway running the length of the sandbox. The take-offs, flights around the room, banking of the plane, and landings were enacted with much care. Mountains of sand kept growing taller as people, vehicles, etc. were buried beneath.

Figure 4.6 Sand scene by Jennifer

Suddenly, some person or thing would erupt violently from a mountain and get back into the action of the scene. Another recurring theme was buried treasure that was eventually "discovered" by workers digging, spadeful by spadeful, until the treasure was revealed.

As her confidence in play increased, Jennifer became a teacher, sometimes a music teacher and at other times a classroom teacher. She was, however, a strict taskmaster and would make the "student" take the tests over and over again until the exercise was done perfectly. With her wicked sense of humor, she changed the criteria constantly. A big feather was tickling punishment for disobedience in class, until you fell down laughing.

After about four weeks, without any warning or preamble, Jennifer began talking spontaneously in sessions. This has now carried over into other areas of her life. Her mother called me afterwards almost in tears, amazed and thankful that this mysterious condition that had frozen her daughter was loosening its grip. Jennifer is now speaking at school at times. She will now read to the teacher and the teacher's assistant, and will ask to be excused to go to the bathroom.

Her mother runs a small business out of their home that must be passed through to get to the family part of the house. Until recently, Jennifer would come in from school, head down and silent, making a beeline through the studio, past her mother's clients. Now she speaks and makes eye contact before heading to the back. (I must not forget to comment upon her beautiful smile that now frequently lights up her face.)

Before beginning play therapy, Jennifer would not participate in any way in sessions at school with the speech therapist who'd tried working with her one-on-one and in small groups. Jennifer would sit or stand rigidly, unable to participate either verbally or non-verbally. For four months I had the speech teacher be part of a weekly play session at school, and that has helped to build their relationship. Jennifer is not yet verbal with the speech therapist, but is much more relaxed, will smile and laugh, make eye contact, shake her head yes or no, play games, put together puzzles, etc. So far she is verbally participating in sessions with the speech therapist, but only with the use of a tape recorder. It is to be hoped that progress will continue this upcoming school year.

Symptoms always serve a function and need to be respected. The inner urge in us humans is toward growth and health. The God within, our "higher self," can be listened to and heeded to promote well-being. With an attuned, empathic play therapist in the safe, protective space that play therapy provides, children who are struggling emotionally, neurologically, or physically can play their way toward greater health and joy.

For me, play therapy continues, after all these years, to be a mysterious and mystical process. It is an honor and an awe-inspiring experience to be allowed to witness, and assist at times, in another's personal journey. "Thank you" to all the children and their families who have allowed me this privilege.

Further reading

Ammann, R. (1991) *Healing and Transformation in Sandplay*. Peru, IL: Open Court Publishing Company.

Baldwin, C. (1994) *Selective Mutism in Children*. London: Whurr Publishers Ltd.

Bradway, K. and McCoard, B. (1997) *Sandplay—Silent Workshop of the Psyche*. New York, NY: Routledge.

Carey, L. (1999) *Sandplay: Therapy with Children and Families*. New Jersey, NJ: Jason Aronson Inc.

Dundas, E. (1978) *Symbols Come Alive in the Sand*. London and Boston, MA: Coventure Ltd.

Kalff, D. (1980) *Sandplay: A Psychotherapeutic Approach to the Psyche*. Boston, MA: Sigo Press.

Landgarten, H. (1981) 'Individual treatment: case history of an elective mute.' In *Clinical Art Therapy, A Comprehensive Guide* (pp.91–104). New York, NY: Brunner/Mazel, Inc.

Maciak, M. (1999) 'A therapy miracle: a mute child speaks!' *International Association for Play Therapy, Inc. Newsletter 18*, 4, 10–11.

McCarthy, D. (1997) 'Awakening the dragon within children.' *Psychological Perspectives 35*, 102–109.

McCarthy, D. (1998) 'Transforming negativity in children.' *Quadrant XXVIII: I*, Winter, 50–60.

McCarthy, D. (2007) *'If You Turned into a Monster.' Transformation through Play: A Body-Centered Approach to Play Therapy.* London: Jessica Kingsley Publishers.

Mitchell, R. and Friedman, H. (1994) *Sandplay: Past, Present and Future.* London and New York, NY: Routledge.

Neumann, E. (1973) *The Child.* New York, NY: G.P. Putnam's Sons.

Spasaro, S. and Schaefer, C. (1999) *Refusal to Speak. Treatment of Selective Mutism in Children.* New Jersey, NJ: Jason Aronson Inc.

Weinrib, E. (1983) *Images of the Self.* Boston, MA: Sigo Press.

Whitmont, E. (1969) *The Symbolic Quest.* Princeton: Princeton University Press.

Chapter 5

The Secret Garden:
Healing through Nature

Ilka List

It is the job of the therapist to loosen the rigidities that rapidly begin to warp a traumatized child's development. One finds that everything has been changed by trauma. The negative impact shows up in play, learning, making friends, relating to parents, and enjoying new experiences, as well as in other ways. Bad experiences make traumatized children think that they are bad people and it was the badness inside that somehow caused the divorce, the abuse, or the abandonment. Although some children are quite verbal and can tell the therapist a lot about what happened, even the most articulate can describe only a certain portion, and perhaps not the most important part. And words of encouragement alone do not provide the needed relief, nor do they usually alter a negative self-perception or an inability in the children to symbolize their feelings and ideas about themselves. I have found that experiences in nature can give children and adults both the means and the metaphors to satisfy some of their inner hunger, provide them with a means to express experiences and conflicts that trouble them, and find a satisfying relief from inner pain.

> As a child, running from the pain of an abusive family situation, Sandra found solace by running through a meadow to the edge of a small pond. There she would throw herself down under an overhanging tree, and spend hours watching the water. As an adult she found herself moving from house to house, and apartment to apartment, until she found one that was located near a pond and a pasture. From her window she could hear ducks quacking and cows mooing, and she finally felt that she could now stay put. She no longer felt the need to move.

My doctoral research into the effects on children of ongoing exploration of the natural world corroborated my observations about how children benefit from being outdoors. Through a complex statistical study of children's artwork, using three independent raters (professionals other than myself who assessed the children's drawings according to specific guidelines), I proved that ongoing experience in nature in the company of an interested and understanding adult had a beneficial effect on children. It gave children who spent time outdoors regularly, having both guided and non-guided experiences, a cognitive boost in terms of spatial relationships and working memory. It also seemed to help them mature slightly earlier emotionally—when their drawings were analyzed we found that children developed an earlier understanding of object constancy. Using several developmental markers, I found that children with extensive outdoor experience did statistically significantly better than their peers who had no such ongoing and guided experience.

This chapter will show how the henhouse, the pond, the garden, and the sandbox (which brings contact with the earth into the playroom) all contribute to children's understanding of the treasures inside themselves. The natural world can provide children with a deeply experienced sense of their own inner life, and a newly supported understanding that their inner world is rich and valuable. It can also help them feel that they are part of a unique and extensive world and that they co-exist alongside other creatures with lives and thoughts of their own, which can be recognized and understood.

My office, which is in my home, is surrounded by an extensive garden. A large pond lies just below the gardens at the bottom of a short, gently sloping lawn. Parents park at the south end of the house, and approach the office with their children through a large gate made of curving cedar boughs which loosely form the simple shape of a large eye. The gate is faded grey in color, and pleasant. It swings open with a light touch to the tinkling sounds of a small set of chimes. Just inside the gate is a long arbor hung with wisteria, trumpet vines, and grapes. The soft, deep, green grass on the path beneath the arbor is bordered on each side by flowerbeds. An espaliered apple tree and pear tree grow heavy with fruit. As the summer progresses, the grapes ripen and become succulent. Children pick them at all stages. "Can I eat this one?" Tony picks a small, hard, bright green grape, and holds it up for me to see. "It's going to be very sour," I tell him. "I like sour," he says and takes a bite. He throws the rest away. Soon the green grapes turn red. They, too, are very sour, but they are less hard. Finally the clusters turn blue. The ripe blue grapes are sweet and delicious. Both coming and going, Tony and his mom stop to pluck handfuls from the vines. The arbor forms a leafy tunnel through which they approach the office.

As five-year-old Sally walked under the arbor she said, "I think you are trying to make a secret garden." "Yes, I am," I replied, thinking back to my childhood when I read Frances H. Burnett's book *The Secret Garden* and felt so deeply moved by it. The story had made a lasting impression on me because it convincingly portrayed the healing power of animals and the nurturing effect of a garden on the troubled young protagonists of the story.

For those who haven't read it, *The Secret Garden* weaves the tale of scrawny, frightened, arrogant, nine-year-old Mary who, when orphaned in India by a plague, is sent to live with her unhappy uncle in a drafty English manor house called Misselthwaite. As the uncle is constantly traveling throughout Europe trying to forget his sorrows, Mary is left to be tended by the house staff and maids, and is consequently very much on her own. From the first night, she hears distant cries and screams echoing through the hallways. Frightened and curious, Mary cautiously creeps along the dark, scary manor house corridors until she discovers the sick room of a willful, disagreeable sick boy, Colin, who is very much Mary's masculine counterpart, close in age yet even more impossible than she. After a number of secret visits to see him, misunderstandings, and violent disagreements, Mary and Colin become friends.

Through Mary's fortuitous discovery of the key to an untended walled garden, overgrown and wild behind a locked door, Mary imagines a project that will benefit both herself and her friends. With some difficulty Mary convinces the insecure Colin to accompany her to the garden, the place where his own mother was killed by a falling tree limb when he was very young. With the help of Dickon, a young friend who is a veritable animal whisperer, and plenty of physical effort (secretly accomplished for the most part), the garden is brought back to serenity and beauty. In its tangled, lost condition the garden is an apt metaphor for all of the emotionally unhappy characters in the story. As the garden shapes up, Mary and Colin rediscover their own good natures, and regain their wholesomeness and health. The story ends with a reunion between Colin and his estranged father who, in being restored to his son and reconciled to the beautiful garden, finds a healing path for himself.

The children in the story are easy to identify with, because they are nasty, whiny, complaining and unreasonable, yet somehow very loveable in their wretchedness. They show all the qualities that parents cannot tolerate, but that children have inside and can't usually reveal. These terrible feelings are part of the monster within. Children badly need to express, accept, and integrate those feelings. Colin, Mary, and Colin's widowed father each have excellent reasons to be unhappy, but as their feelings are locked away unacknowledged, each character does many things that hurt other people. As the story opens they are all stuck in their pain and haven't a clue about how to help themselves feel better.

The Secret Garden describes a remarkable solution to a seemingly hopeless state of affairs. Healing comes in two ways: first, through their deepening relationship to animals with the perfect help of Dickon, and second, by developing a relationship to the natural world and to each other through working hard together in the garden. The story provides each of the characters with a way to deal with the out-of-control emotions that resulted from terrible troubles that wreaked havoc on their lives. The children heal themselves with the help of the natural world, and the kind acts of some of the staff of Misselthwaite. And in healing themselves the children create a way to heal the troubled heart of Colin's father. To resolve the pain they feel, the children have to challenge some unproductive attitudes in themselves, and learn to work together to transform the wildness of the secret garden into something spiritually nourishing. The book makes a powerful suggestion that healing comes from action and mutuality, neither from the wise suggestions of others, nor from the process of putting all their bad feelings into words (Burnett 1909).

It was years before I understood the powerful impact of The Secret Garden on my life. Yet I can see how the healing found in that storybook garden made me want to create my own secret garden. Surely it would be wonderful to have a garden with an impenetrable stone wall, accessible only through a secret door, just like the garden in the story, but I am satisfied that the passage through my long cedar arbor, and the potential meaning of the vegetable garden, the henhouse, and the pond all provide a sense of mystery and hopefulness.

A vegetable garden with inviting lettuce, green beans, and tomatoes can be seen through a little gate off one side of the arbor. Once I show children the tomatoes and green beans, they run in and out through the gate and pick food for themselves. Free access to the vegetable garden and to the arbor tells children, "This is a nourishing place for you. You can find delicious things to eat here and you can pick them for yourself." It teaches without words the abundance of nature, the pleasures of gathering food for oneself, and the joy of independence.

Peggy never knew, before she visited the garden, that strawberries came from plants in a garden. She always thought they just came in boxes from the store. Once she discovered them in their row, she picked them and ate them every visit. Her joy triggered a responsive and joyful chord in her father, who was reminded of his own childhood pleasure in picking things in a garden. Their shared experience in the garden contributed to a new closeness between them.

Many children have never had the satisfaction of picking a green bean or a grape straight off the vine, and they need this firsthand evidence to convince them of the nurturing aspect of the environment. These good experiences lay in sharp contrast to the natural disasters pictured on TV of thunderstorms, earthquakes, tornadoes, floods, and hurricanes, and the frightening visions of predation on the nature shows. "Is this where green beans come from?" asked Sam, opening a long green pod to reveal the huge white beans inside. "Can I eat one of these tomatoes?" asks Sally. Many children can hardly believe that food comes from fields, gardens, trees, and bushes.

There is an intriguing complexity in a garden. The variety of vegetation—leaves, vines, and flowering plants of many sizes, shapes, colors, and descriptions—tickles the mind to try and comprehend all the shapes and sizes. Children can experience flashing, dancing patterns of light and shade created by the leaves as the sun pours through the spaces between them. They can pick insects from blossoms, and flowers from stems. They can feel the impact of a view over the pond and the security of sheltering branches. They can investigate strange pods, and listen to birds' calls and the hum of insects. They can hear and feel the wind whispering through the branches and leaves. Touching, smelling, hearing, sensing, children grow curious, animated, and joyful with all their senses, leaping and awakened. This delightful bombardment on the senses from sources that have been a part of our natural environment since we first walked on Earth, can be summed up with the words *simultaneous perception*. As creatures, it is the kind of experience we both crave and need. And it can only be found out of doors.

Early childhood exploration of the natural world is developmentally significant for the brain. With this kind of stimulation, more neurons are used and complex pathways are set up in response to the wonderful variety of stimulating sights, sounds, and smells. It is very possible that some of the neurons that come into play in response to these stimuli are kept when the brain cleans house (around seven, and again in adolescence) and sloughs off unwanted, unused cells. All of the experiences gained with delight through simultaneous perception in the outdoors add richness and depth to children's inner world.

As clients continue under the arbor towards my office they see a leafy passageway and a small cedar gate that stands open and inviting. They pass from the shadowy arbor into the blazing sunlight. The difference in temperature can be startling. Suddenly, the sheltering aspect of the arbor takes on a new significance.

When children are around eight years old, shelter-building becomes a favorite activity. Wherever they build one, children enjoy making a home of their own. Some lucky children have access to the woods, fields of long grass, evergreen trees with drooping boughs, bushes with low arching branches, or trees with low sturdy branches. City children build their special places under tables and beds and behind couches in the house. Some use chairs and blankets, or even umbrellas, to create a shelter. Some build with blocks, or make miniature imaginary worlds in the sand tray in the playroom. In his wonderful book *Children's Special Places*, David Sobel explores children's developmental stages in relation to the natural world (Sobel 1993). Sobel found that most children show an interest in building forts, huts, or some other kind of shelter—an important step towards achieving a sense of themselves as beings separate from their parents. Much of their play in and around their hideouts is an imaginative exploration of their independence. They are playing at making their way in the world. They are finding out how they feel, what they like; in general, who they are when they are on their own.

Another kind of shelter was constructed in a winter nature-exploration program for adolescents who had been hospitalized for obesity and diabetes. Clay was offered as the afternoon activity. Sixteen-year-old Michael took a small, flat rectangle (about three inches by four inches) of clay and at first was totally unsure about what to do with it. Then he got busy and added a multitude of tiny twigs to the perimeter, creating a miniature image of a sheltered glade. In the open center, surrounded by the tiny trees, he laid a small, moss-covered piece of bark. It looked like a wee bench or couch. It was easy to imagine just such a place in the real forest, a beautiful, hidden, safe place, all that could be desired in a hideout. I asked Michael if he had ever built a hideout in his neighborhood. "Yes, in my friend's backyard," he said. He kept looking proudly at his creation, and brought his friends over to admire its beauty. Symbolically, it represented a real forest glade to which Michael could imaginatively return again and again when he felt the need.

The concept of a safe shelter, whether life-size or miniature, a shelter that can protect and hide you, yet offers openings through which to look into the world around, is a valuable imaginative inner asset for both children and adults. The secret garden described above is just such a container. But even as an act of imagination, the shelter of the daydream or visualization provides a sense of protection, peace, and solitude. The imaginative shelter may have windows, spy holes, or gaps in the walls. It may not be closed in at all. It allows for a most satisfying flow of feelings and experience, in and out. But all kinds of shelters, the real shelter or bush hut, the enclosed garden, the miniature woodland glade, and the imaginative shelter that exists only in the mind, make the outer world of nature, with its plethora of people, animals, wild plants, woods, gardens, and fields, tempting to explore. The sheltered, contained person can choose just how much contact to permit with the outer world and can beat a retreat into their hideout when it's necessary.

For traumatized children it may take some tentative forays and retreats from the hideout before they are relaxed enough to explore the surroundings of the hideout freely. Dr Santostefano in his book *Child Therapy in the Great Outdoors* (2004) describes children emerging and retreating over many weeks or even months as they learn to trust the protective qualities of the shelter and meet the challenge of the world at large, a world they initially see as dangerous. The feeling of being sheltered in a safe yet permeable container fills a common psychological need. A hideout is also a perfect metaphor for ourselves, our bodies being our shelters and our eyes, the windows.

Inside my office, a large friendly old dog and a Maine coon cat greet children. The dog allows the children to pet her and feed her treats in return for tricks, and the cat permits one or two of the children to throw him over their shoulders and cart him around. Despite the good nature of the dog, some children are afraid of her. "Get him away from me, I hate dogs!" screamed a nine-year-old, still coping with many fears, and as yet unable to distinguish a friendly dog from a dangerous one. For children who are afraid of animals, the dog and cat are shut out of the way. They are brought back on the scene only when the children decide to try and become more comfortable with them. Dog biscuits and doggie tricks sometimes help to break the ice and inspire confidence in a timid child.

Near the office/house is the "chicken palace" with its large and sturdy outdoor pen. It has a strong wood and wire gate, through which we take the hens treats of corn and green vegetables. The hens scratch, peck, dig, and take dustbaths in holes they have carved in the dirt floor of the pen. The hens constantly watch for someone coming from the house, and when they spy us they beg for food with loud, demanding cries. Some children are a bit scared of the talkative birds, which squawk meaningfully and shrilly for the treats they expect. Slowly children get used first to touching and then to holding the friendliest birds. It seems that the chickens fascinate most people, and if they ever had one as a pet, their faces light up with delight at the memory. Bold children chase the hens around, trying to catch and hold one of them.

Sara dashed around the coop trying to corner Golden Pantaloon, a fluffy yellow bird with feathers on her feet. She scooted under the low branches of the lilac bush and cherry tree, and then cornered the hen inside the palace where roosts and nest boxes await the hens' use in the quiet interior of the building. Sara grabbed Pantaloon by the feet, despite the hen's loud screeching and flapping. Pantaloon settled down into Sara's arms and relaxed. She was kissed and patted.

It was a different matter for Peggy. When Peggy first came to see me, she looked like a well put-together child, self-confident and secure. It was hard to imagine her problems, although I soon discovered that she was just waiting for me to turn my back so that she could throw something at me, or otherwise hurt me. One day on her way into the office Peggy grabbed my hand and led me to the gatepost. Eagerly she put out her arms to a large Rhode Island Red hen that was sitting on top of it. The hen hunkered down into a fluffy ball when I picked her up. I tried to put her in Peggy's eager arms. But Peggy was unable to fold her arms around the hen's body, and I discovered the extent of Peggy's rigidity in this way. Trembling, she held her arms out, stiff and unbending. But although Peggy could not bear to hold the hen yet, she was immensely pleased to have touched its soft feathers.

Before her next session I happened to find a small painted turtle. I kept it to show her. Peggy held the turtle despite its sharp claws and turned it this way and that, amazed at the intriguing colored patterns on its head, neck, and legs. Then she painted a picture of it. Images of turtles were included in every subsequent drawing and painting, for holding the turtle had represented an important gain in Peggy's personal courage, and demonstrated a new level of trust in me. At her next session Peggy was not afraid to hold a hen. After she placed it gently down she proudly collected eggs for her whole family. As Peggy gained confidence she began to ask me to collaborate with her on some of her paintings. We talked about colors, textures, and patterns, working pleasurably side by side. Peggy's sneaky and hurtful behavior dropped away.

The biggest treat for clients of all ages is collecting eggs. They are treasures for children, but also for their parents. Everyone I work with is eager to discover eggs in the nest boxes.

Warren, an autistic boy, with an irresistible compulsion to count, was eager to hold a hen. But when Zebra flapped and screeched, Warren screamed angrily at me, "Don't you see that she doesn't like what you are doing?" Collecting eggs, however, made him dance with joy, and he took home all the eggs that he found. An egg is a magic little item, symbolic of so much. In that one small form we contain the idea of new beginnings, mysteries, the generation of new life, new feelings, new possibilities, and new ideas. It is a symbol used by the major religions to convey the sacred quality of new beginnings. No one is immune to its fresh radiance.

Eight-year-old Anna wanted to spend all of her therapy sessions in the henhouse, taming the hens. Anna was temperamentally unable to accommodate herself to anyone's schedule, whether at school or at home. She was under tremendous pressure to measure up, and an hour in the henhouse allowed her to relax and become self-directive. When I became tired of so much time in the chicken coop, Anna and I explored the land around the pond. Then, back in the playroom, Anna made an elaborate scene in the sandbox portraying the pond we had just explored. Her imaginary scene had the vivid, glowing quality of a sacred place.

When I saw Anna again at fifteen because of problems stemming from the academic pressures of high school, she did not want to talk to me or any other adults. "I talk to my friends about everything, so I don't need to talk with you," she told me. But if I asked her about her pet cats, she told me enthusiastically all about their behavior, and how one was smarter than the other. As a gifted observer of animal behavior, Anna had noticed that one cat made up simple games to amuse itself, while the other did not. Outside she took dozens of digital photos of the pond, the fields, and the trees. In nature, in the chicken coop, and in the sandbox, Anna was relaxed and whole. In every other place, except with her friends, she was guarded and watchful. With a child so unwilling to talk about her ideas and feelings, it was significant to me to discover that there are still many things that she loves and values. But I only found this out by talking with her about animals or by going outside with her to explore nature.

Below the house is a large pond. Sometimes we take nets with long green handles down to the pond, and probe its depths. With special permission from the parents, I take some children out in the canoe, to fish or drag the nets. The pond with its dark and clay-filled water has a mysterious quality. It is fascinating to scoop things up from below.

> During her last weeks of therapy, when Anita had finished her scrambled eggs, we would go to the pond edge and dip for creatures. We have found fish, young turtles, and dragonfly nymphs. Most significant for Anita were the freshwater clams of all sizes that she dragged up and lined up on the grassy bank of the pond. Each one was very heavy and very much alive. "Look!" she would tell me, "here is another, and it's bigger that the last. Look how huge it is!" The clam must have weighed well over a pound, and it made the smallest clam look very tiny. All of the bivalves were obstinately shut. Nothing would make them open until we placed them in a tub of water.
>
> Then slowly and tentatively, the two shells would part and a soft, pale foot would emerge, probing the water, trying to find a way to dig down into some mud. "What is it doing? What is that thing?" Anita asked. Then she said, "Look at the shiny part with the rainbow colors!" She directed me to look at the hinge on each clam. An iridescent, bare space of shell surrounded each hinge. "That's mother-of-pearl," I told her. To me it is a treasure. The pond is full of wonderful treasures. Feeling a little awkward and unsure, I added, "You have treasures inside of you too, hidden away but still there, just like in the pond." I felt a bit self-conscious saying this, but Anita was nearly twelve by now, and she easily understood what I was saying. I said a little more, "You have surprising thoughts, and ideas, and beautiful feelings too, deep down inside you, just waiting to be found and netted." "And some ugly ones too," she told me.
>
> Anita continued her exploration and expressed excitement with everything she found. Towards the last she pulled up an antique inkwell. The light green glass and old-fashioned shape gave her a big thrill. "Someone must have lost this a long, long time ago!" she exclaimed. Then all at once, the inkwell sprang out of her hands. It landed back in the pond and we couldn't find it again, even though we waded into the mud in the shallow water and probed here and there. "But I got to see it!" she said. "And I will find it again someday."

Experiences in nature can help a child develop a theory of mind. We want to see children begin to understand that people and other animals have thoughts and feelings that are their own. Children can begin to relate to others as separate, interesting beings. It is important for all of us to gain this understanding. Dabbling in the depths of a pond brings creatures to light that are new and different to children's eyes, living organisms unlike themselves in every way, yet still living. Recognizing otherness is a challenge for us all, but experience in nature makes that otherness vividly clear and exciting. It is almost incomprehensible that even the smallest freshwater shrimp has microscopic muscles controlling its movements through the water. Children can look at a shrimp, or a dragonfly naiad, and under-stand—it has muscles, and I have muscles, but we are very different. Children can ask questions such as: What makes a clam a living creature when it looks and feels like a rock? Why does it resist prying open when it is brought out of the water? How does it know things? What does it eat?

By trying to comprehend other forms of life, children at the same moment define themselves. I don't live under water. I don't have two hard shells. My muscles are under my skin, not hidden beneath a shell or a carapace. I don't have gills like a fish. As these differences become apparent, each newly discovered animal helps a child know more about himself or herself. Significant questions are asked, such as: What am I like? What do I hope for? Need I be afraid? How can I become brave? What does it mean to be alive? What is death? All of the most meaningful questions of life spring naturally out of contact with nature.

Natural phenomena provide metaphors for certain human conditions and emotional states. Without ever having tried to wedge open a clam and felt its resistance to pressure, how can any of us know what it means to clam up, to refuse to tell what one needs to tell? Slow as a turtle, quick as a bunny, slippery as an eel—all of these phrases, and many more, have their applica-tions to human life. While helping us to describe our behavior, or ourselves, they also bring poetry into these simple descriptions of our lives. Each phrase that describes us with an image drawn from the behavior of an animal or the quality of plant life reminds us of our connection to the natural world. And we are also described in terms of geology: "He had a stony expression" —and weather: "I stormed around the house until I was no longer angry." These metaphors are important because they reaffirm our connection to nature. And remind us that we are just one part of the great world.

Of course there are many different kinds of environments, and people live in very different places. Each of these places becomes the context for metaphors to describe us. It is certain that metaphors from a desert, a moun-tainside, or a forest differ from those drawn from grassland. They come out of centuries of observation of certain similarities between human behavior and the natural world. They are far from literal descriptions. Contrast "She walked very slowly" with the phrase "She moved along at a snail's pace." If one knows snails and how they move, the kind of slowness that the girl exhibited becomes fuller and richer in meaning. Often a metaphor pulled from the natural world is the best way of describing our behavior and actions. It is interesting to contrast these phrases with descriptions drawn from technology.

There is a vast array of sensory perceptions out of doors in a wild environment. They come flooding into the self from leaves, the ground, grass, water, small plants and towering trees, wind, clouds, sun, and rain. They pour into us through our eyes, our ears, our noses, and our mouths. The sounds and smells stimulate us and orient us to the place in which we stand. We respond to the feeling of the solid ground under our feet, a piece of grass in our fingers, our body weight and position in space. All these sensations are part of the wonder of being alive. These complex perceptions, even though they are received simultaneously, do not overwhelm a child, but are usually calming and full of joy. And the consequence of the experience is that the child feels a profound sense of being a creature in a particular place, the right kind of place, one that brings good feelings. Children with their feet on the forest floor and sticks in their hands, with a path before them to follow to an unknown destination, are filled with the pleasure of fitting into the world, of having somewhere to go and something to do. In these times when people move from state to state, city to city, and country to country, it is especially important for a child to know how to connect with the natural world and feel they belong there, in a place of diversity, continuity, and fascinating possibilities.

Because children's thought processes and feelings are more like the simultaneous experiences they have in nature than they are like narratives, the best expression of their feelings and thoughts is in clusters of images that portray their experiences all together in a group, and not word by word, one following the other. There is much to be said for an idea developed by Margaret Lowenfeld in *World Play* (Lowenfeld 1929) [AQ]. She maintained that children process their experiences with *cluster thinking*, and that because they think that way it is difficult for them to express complex kinds of experiences. Traumatic experiences are especially difficult. Grounding in the natural world, as described in the preceding paragraphs, in conjunction with the creation of images in the therapist's sandbox, can provide children with new experiences, ideas, similes, and metaphors that can help them express and begin to resolve the unspeakable.

References

Burnett, F.H. (1909) *The Secret Garden.* Portsmouth: Heineman.

Lowenfeld, M. (2005) *Understanding Children's Sandplay: Lowenfeld's World Technique.* Eastbourne: Sussex Academic Press.

Santostefano, S. (2004) *Child Therapy in the Great Outdoors.* New Jersey, NJ and London: The Analytic Press.

Sobel, D. (1993) *Children's Special Places: Exploring the Role of Forts, Dens, and Bush Houses in Middle Childhood.* Tucson, AZ: Zephyr Press.

Further reading

Cobb, E. (1959) *The Ecology of Imagination in Childhood.* Boston, MA: American Academy of Arts and Sciences.

List, A. and List, I. (1977) *A Walk in the Forest.* New York, NY: Crowell.

List, I. (1962) *Let's Explore the Shore.* New York, NY: Obolensky.

List, I. (1970) *Questions and Answers about Seashore Life.* New York, NY: Four Winds Press.

List, I. (1975) *Grandma's Beach Surprise.* New York, NY: Putnam.

List, I. (1994) 'On evaluating environmental education.' In L.A. Stringer and Ewert (eds) *Coalition for Education in the Outdoors. Special Research Symposium Proceedings.* Bradford Woods, IN: Coalition for Education in the Outdoors.

List, I. (1998) *The Impact of Environmental Context and Programmed Nature Study on Children's Art. An Analysis of Content and Structure in 1,872 Drawings by Second and Third Grade Children.* UMI Dissertation Services, 300 North Zeeb Road. P.O. Box a1346, Ann Arbor, MI 48106-1346, USA.

List, I. (2002) *Moths and Butterflies of North America.* New York, NY: Franklin Watts.

Louv, R. (2005) *Last Child in the Woods: Saving Our Children from Nature Deficit Disorder.* Chapel Hill, NC: Algonquin Books.

Mitchell, J.H. (2001) *The Wildest Place on Earth: Italian Gardens and the Invention of Wilderness.* Washington, DC: Counterpoint Press of Perseus Books Group.

Chapter 6

Speaking with the Imagination

Patti Knoblauch

The words, "Nothing happens unless first a dream," by the renowned American poet Carl Sandburg (1970, p.282) provide the caption to a picture of a child building a sandcastle on the beach, which is displayed on a shelf in my play therapy office. If we take the dream to be only one manifestation of the imagination, we can understand that nothing happens unless first the imagination, whether it finds expression in dream, story, drama, demeanor, movement, visual art, sand, or any form. From my experience as a therapist, I am willing to concede that nothing happens *without* the imagination, given the nature of human consciousness; however, the imagination may not *always* be out in front. Often, though, it does lead the way to change, and it behooves the therapist to at least be aware of it, and at best be in relationship with the imagination as much as with the conscious functioning of the client.

In this chapter, the selected exposition of one child's play therapy sessions is shared with the intent to show the vital role, the power and centrality of imagination to spur and to create change and healing. Superficially, his expressions appear as stories, dramatizations, and scenes in the sandbox or on the floor. More deeply, his imaginative explorations help bring about change, much as taking a journey affects and changes us in ways mapping the journey can only imply.

Curiously, I sometimes felt as though I did not know what I was doing. It became clear from my attention to the child's process that, in fact, I was not doing. He was doing, and among other drives within him, his imagination was doing. I was facilitating his doing. He was the central figure of his process, in charge, needing from me sometimes a nod of assent, sometimes more encouragement to go in directions which may not have been as welcome in his reality outside of therapy. In this culture, we often need reminders and even guidance to know what is safe in the imagination, and then again to know how we can safely express our imagination. As a therapist, it is my job to watch and tend to those boundaries.

This child's therapeutic process, in particular, exemplifies the force and value of imagination in therapy, because, for the most part, his imagination was healthy. It was his physical health which was challenged and which led to his psychological challenges.

Case study: Jack

Jack was diagnosed with Barth's syndrome, a developmental syndrome which delays physical development by three to four years, and can impair immune functioning. Jack required unusual medical intervention as early as in his first week of life. Jack attended play therapy from ages 9 to 12 and returned briefly at age 13. At age 9, he was held back in school and was confronting practical, social, and emotional challenges associated with his delayed development. Previously seen by his parents as brave, strong, and confident, he began to show clear signs of clinginess and insecurity.

Jack was growing up in an intact family, with devoted, involved, sensitive and informed parents and two siblings, who were supportive of his developmental and special needs. Jack's parents brought him to therapy because they felt he needed an opportunity to talk about his disease, his feelings about who he was, and to explore what the disease meant to him. Like so many children and adults, Jack did not show any interest in talking about his feelings and very little interest in talking about his disease. This was no different in therapy. As therapy proceeded, Jack did open up and talk about his feelings with his parents at home. In therapy, however, he would acknowledge his feelings only if the subject was brought up by his parents or therapist. Otherwise, his interest lay in speaking through the imagination.

In Jack's first session, he was practically mute, except for some barely audible narration in response to my narration of his play. He played like this, without speech, in many sessions. In later stages of therapy he played for most of the session setting up scenes that led to a few dramatic moments at the end. During the set-up he remained silent, and requested that I hold my questions and comments until the drama was unfolded. Then he told in words what we were witnessing, as we watched many seemingly unbelievable events together. Sometimes Jack prepared for a dramatic moment over the course of more than one session, such as when he created a large "boulder" out of clay to destroy a figure representing a particularly irritating and frustrating adult, who in his everyday life he was required to interact with respectfully. He waited for the clay to dry between sessions, so that it would be hard and dense enough to deliver a satisfying blow to the clay figure representing the adult.

Jack came to therapy with a quiet verbal voice but bursting with impulses to play. From the first session, he engaged various types of mediums and spread his play around the room, using floor, sandbox, doll's house, blocks, and the table with art materials. He allowed himself the freedom to engage the materials, as if his relationship with them was grounded in trust. These are hallmarks of health in a child: freedom to take up space, to use materials to serve self-expression and drama, and to trust the materials enough to be open to what happens when one interacts with them. It was almost as if he were putting himself into them, and in unison, things happen and change.

I observed Jack's use of, and interactions with, the play materials as shamanic. The shaman, the medicine person in indigenous cultures, is a healer. The shamanic method is one of participation with nature. It could be said that all of indigenous culture is participatory in method, because in order to survive and thrive indigenous cultures were required to know how to fit comfortably within their overwhelming natural environments. The shaman is seen as the expert on this, known to have a foot in both worlds, that of the everyday popular world and that of the spirit world. The shaman serves as a bridge to join what seems disparate or separate, in order to integrate, to re-establish the felt experience of wholeness which is always present, and to heal by his or her pronounced capacities to be receptive enough to allow and participate in the mysteries of healing. Jack's shamanic use of materials was evidenced in his openness to the play materials in order to follow his journeys to their mysterious and satisfying outcomes.

The source of the shaman's power is in his or her relationship with nature and the spirit world. The source of power is not a set of techniques. Similarly with Jack, mysterious, creative, and wonderful things poured forth from his imaginative play, along with surprises and reasons for hope. In Jack's imagination, magic was an acceptable way of getting things to happen. He referenced it openly and resorted to it matter-of-factly, not as though he were using a technique, but as though he were granting a nod of assent to the powers of change in the imaginative world, which is bigger than his conscious awareness and has different boundaries.

Jack played spontaneously, because he brought to therapy a functioning imagination that allowed him creativity, mystery, and healing. Yet Jack needed and used therapy to feel better, because he needed to be able to use his bursting impulses, his creative imagination, his capacities to contemplate and participate in the mysteries of life, and his latent reservoir of healing, in order to find his personal meaning for all he had gone through in life. He needed to find this meaning and to begin to tell his story in his own personal way. He already knew his story through the eyes of his doctors, through the words of his parents, through his community in the Barth Foundation, of which he and his family were active members. But information, even support and loving care, are not always enough for the human psyche. As human beings moving from one stage of development to the next, our awareness shifts and our perspective changes. Around age nine, there is a distinct growth of awareness and self-consciousness, which is popularly noted as pre-adolescence or sometimes the "tweens." Children are observed to become more aware of their appearance, although not as much as in the early teens, when adolescence really sets in. Awareness of social networks is another big step around age nine for both girls and boys. That is why, when Jack hit age nine, his story as seen through the eyes of his doctors, his parents, and the Barth community no longer sustained him.

The awareness began to dawn on him that he was expected, and felt drawn to be, his own agent, and he was going to have to find ways of doing that even with his physical delays. It is not an easy task for a nine-year-old who is three years physically delayed to enter into the competitive, self-conscious, and socially hungry world with his peers successfully, but Jack, with his healthy family background and imagination, was determined to do so. Thus, he was as worried and shy as he was equally mischievous and commanding. In addition to needing to tell his story in his own personal pre-adolescent voice, another of the tasks of Jack's therapy was to find a comfortable relationship between the inhibiting and the assertive aspects of himself.

Jack's play was self-directed. For the first year-and-a-half I wrote notes during sessions, occasionally and upon his request reading back to him a narrative he had dictated. He seemed to enjoy a feeling of being center-stage. Then he asked me to stop taking notes, and I did. This was around the time he began to play at imaginatively making movies, which is discussed later in this chapter. It seemed to me he had achieved a more complex sense of himself, which may have felt to him as though he was able to participate as all the characters in the movies, as writer, director and producer of the movies, and as audience, or witness, as well. Indeed a sophisticated accomplishment for (at that point) a ten-year-old, but possible in a child with the resources that Jack had. I sometimes asked clarifying questions, but we *never* interpreted or analyzed his play!

That being said, I observed and followed from the first session three themes that Jack was working with in his play. These themes he revisited, and seemed to need the extra attention afforded by therapy in order to feel comfortable with in his being, that is, within his psyche and body, in order to continue to meet his developmental challenges with the confidence and joy which his parents had described of him as a younger child. I refer to these themes as "nurturing," "surviving," and "conquering," to honor the imaginative landscapes that Jack provides as their context. Over the course of play sessions, *nurturance* is often seen in food, protection, and medical care. *Survival* is seen in near misses, injuries, deaths, and rebirths. *Conquering* is seen as getting the treasure, and in the end as Jack's ability to imagine that he frankly wins, he is frankly victorious, even at the expense of another, painfully difficult as that may be to imagine in a child as sensitive as Jack.

The following is a synopsis of his play in the first session:

Jack begins at the doll's house, focussing on the dogs. He gives the dogs a shower, feeds them a peanut butter and jelly sandwich, and then takes the shower to the sandbox. He chooses a shark from the shelves of sandplay miniatures and showers the shark in the sandbox. He returns to the shelves, visually exploring the selection of objects. He picks out fences, four tan soldiers and one green one, a tank, and boats. He plays soldiers on the floor next to the sandbox. The green soldier finds treasure, and then is attacked. Jack gets blocks, and using pretend tools, builds shelters. He takes the soldier to the hospital in a toy ambulance. Jack says the soldier was "that close to getting home"—showing me how close with his fingers. A friend visits the soldier in the hospital, and is attacked on the way. The friend hides the treasure in a "home" Jack had built. Jack then announces he wants to "make something," and he paints an American flag which fills the paper.

The aforementioned themes of nurturing, surviving, and conquering are established in Jack's first play scene. He is drawn to the "house" at first, where he engages in the nurturing play of caring for the dog. Jack has two sisters, one younger and one older, and was very familiar with this kind of play at home. But nurturing in Jack's life represents more than just child's play. Being three years delayed in physical development and requiring serious medications to stabilize his heart, and shots every other day in his stomach region to boost his immune system, Jack was in many ways receiving nurturance above and beyond that of a typical child, even given the loving environment of his family.

This situation posed a challenge to Jack, who at nine years of age was faced with naturally growing impulses to independence. Might the shark who replaces the dog as the recipient of bathing reflect an image which Jack uses to show how it feels to him, or how he imagines it feels, to grow from a dependent, domesticated, servile or cooperative, cute little object into a more powerful, assertive—indeed aggressive—being who will still require care? The incongruity of a shark being showered in a shower stall suggests a puzzle Jack has to solve regarding growing up and dependency needs, as well as reconciling aggression and domestication or acculturation. Ultimately, Jack uses his therapy to work all this out, and in so doing he broadens his concepts of both dependency and independence. This transformation is not merely intellectual, for it is achieved through Jack's imaginative explorations of the roles of nurturer, survivor, and conqueror, through his play.

In Jack's first play scene, both the soldier who finds the treasure and his friend are attacked. Jack's use of his fingers to show how close the first soldier had been to getting home emphasizes to me that the experience of nearly but not quite making it is in his body. I work with the assumption that all of Jack's creations emanate from his body experience, but I understand that nearly making it and maybe not making it may be particularly charged experiences for Jack. Jack is telling and playing about surviving. Finally, the theme of conqueror is introduced by Jack's drawing of the American flag. This choice suggests much more than superiority. It also suggests unity, identity, and rightful place, as well as national treasure to Jack, whose family had been personally touched by 9/11, just one year before.

> Jack steps into the room on his second visit and announces "What we need is a bird." Giving his voice to an army figure he adds, "A bird to protect us." Having found a bird, the army figure explains to the bird its mission, that for a year it is to wake up every morning and state whether to expect an attack that day or not. During that time the bird can expect to be fed one time, with 600 pounds of food. Jack sets up an army base scene. All go to sleep, and along comes the first attacker, a cat. The bird cries out, and the army man throws the cat away, saying, "That's it, cat, you're going." The cat ends up in the garbage truck, on base, with the army man saying, "Alright, but if you hurt her (the bird), that's it."

With incredible self-assertion and self-assurance, Jack chooses a bird to sound the alarm for an army base. Birds are known to signal danger in underground mines; however, their reputation as "protectors" in any other sense is the child of Jack's imagination.

As I watched this scene unfold, I felt dumbfounded, almost sad, wondering how such a tiny, timid creature as a bird could fulfill its charge. I felt it had been set up unfairly, and with the advance of the cat, I felt sure it was doomed to disappoint the army commander, as well as meet its own demise in its inevitable failure. As Jack told the story, his demeanor too was sad and low.

But Jack had tricked me as well as the cat, and in his magician-like performance, he allowed the bird success. By using its voice, within the interdependent community of the army base, the bird's alarm was recognized and heeded, and all were allowed to survive, including the sneaky and predatory cat. Jack created a story and scene wherein the vulnerable creature is elevated to a position of importance and responsibility, which it can fulfill if supported by its community. The community provides the nurturance—600 pounds of food (!)—a timely and effective response, so that the vulnerable creature with its overbearing responsibility can emerge empowered and a hero.

Jack's announcement "What we need is a bird" hints at comedy, tragedy, magic, and poetry, both as a surprising opening line of the second session, and as Jack unveils the bird's dubious role in the beginning of the drama. In creating the drama, Jack himself becomes the nurturer and the nurtured and the survivor. He begins to solve the problem of how to be domestic yet wield power and aggression. Indeed, in the following session, Jack puts forth two focal stories. One is about a baby on a camping trip with its mother, who has to be rushed to the hospital. And another about the bird on top of their tent, who, while everyone sleeps, goes out in the world and makes mischief.

In his imagination, through the figure of the empowered bird, Jack can begin to explore the role of mischief-maker which, as developmentally challenged, had been difficult for him as a younger child due to his needs for sustained protection and nurturance. The role of mischief-maker can potentially pose a threat to the younger child's needs to be identified as dependent and in need of protection.

In the next session (the fourth), Jack became a pizza maker, whom I named "the master pizza chef." I called Jack "the master pizza chef" over and over as this role developed over several sessions, and as Jack's interest in preparing food at home expanded. In his real life, Jack liked to help prepare meals for his family and to assist his grandmother on holidays and special occasions, and now was even beginning to prepare complete dinners for his family.

Jack's performance as pizza chef was a sight to behold! He prepared all kinds of pizza dough, mixing clay, sand, and water, in different proportions, fixing toppings, arranging special pizza ovens and warming trays, employing a rolling pin and implements such as paintbrushes and pencils to design the pizza, setting up a delivery service with trucks, cars, telephones, and signs. He assigned me the role of assistant, about which I went on and on, saying how honored I was to be his assistant in making all his customers so satisfied with his pizza. Although he pleased and delighted his customers no end (in his imaginative descriptions and dramatizations), the master pizza chef didn't have it easy. He had to work very hard to keep up with all the pizza requests, to prove himself, to keep his reputation and to deal with the numerous rude and unruly customers. One couldn't help feeling that Jack must have felt something at least similar amid his peers, though this was never uttered. He showed enormous dedication and pride in his accomplishments! In contrast to Jack's demeanor while setting up the bird as sentinel, Jack's demeanor as master pizza chef was expansive and exuberant.

Over the next several sessions, in addition to pizza chef, Jack played out several stories that expressed more outgoing energy and bravado. With respect to his home life, Jack's mother consulted me about a few mischievous incidents and inappropriate behavior that Jack had become involved in with other children. I encouraged and supported her in setting limits, which Jack seemed to accept with relief. Mischief in the imagination is not, after all, synonymous with mischief in the real world! Jack was venturing into the new and exciting lands of children making their own rules with other children and pressing them against those of the adults, but he readily accepted the boundaries.

In therapy, Jack's exploration of aggression continued through his imagination, using several different plots. In one session he created the image of a monstrous man, as he called it, that wanted to destroy the earth and everyone on it. There were several battles, including one in which he enjoyed squirting me with water from a quart-sized spray bottle of water.

Nurturance took a back seat to survival in these scenes, and survival took on an added dimension of having numerous lives, or being able to live for hundreds and thousands of years after being buried or sealed underground or in a contained area. As in the very first play scene, where a soldier who gets the treasure is attacked and needs to be taken to the hospital in an ambulance, the ambulance and the hospital continued to be present in the majority of Jack's scenes.

There can be little doubt that Jack's experience of his own health and his reliance on his own body was fraught with ambivalence. He agreeably welcomed the support of his medical community, including routine testing and measuring, and inoculations, and he knew that he had been given last rites following congestive heart failure on his second day of life. In his daily life this very year in gym, he experienced difficulty keeping up with his peers, shortness of breath, and tiredness of muscles. Yet he loved to run around and play and to resurrect himself from almost everything. I believe that Jack's explorations of aggression in therapy helped him reconcile his ambivalence about aggression in many ways, as well as having helped him mobilize his own aggression to put in the service of transforming his identity at this critical developmental juncture of pre-adolescence.

During this phase of Jack's therapy, I talked to his parents about the importance of Jack having father–son time. Although Jack's father, a tall, sturdily built man, was a solid family provider and an involved husband and father, Jack's mother was also a provider. Additionally, she held a position of significant responsibility in the medical field, and it was from her side of the family that Barth's syndrome was passed. She was educated, capable, and managed Jack's medical schedule. Traditionally, she took Jack and his sisters, along with family friends, on a camping trip each summer. Jack's parents appeared to present in traditional gender roles, but acknowledged more of a matriarchal bent to the family atmosphere. Jack's father joked about Jack wanting to use his father's tools, of which he had very few. While it took time to evolve, father–son time and a special father–son trip, which with my encouragement Jack had asked for and planned with his father, did occur, and was proudly marked with photos they shared with me, and most likely will be fondly remembered by Jack. A part of the identity Jack was forging concerned being a boy growing up into a man like his father.

Jack's imagination was the driver of his explorations of his aggression in his therapy. Jack's participation in his aggressive explorations was key to allowing his relationship to aggression—to aggressive feelings within himself as well as aggression in his outer world, including between peers and what he knew about aggression between countries—to transform, to allow him to witness aggression, to be in its presence, to think about it, and to know and take his own stance without becoming anxious, covering his anxiety with bravado, and regressing to the more dependent position of his younger years, in relation to his parents and siblings at home.

As Jack moved through the themes of nurturance and survival in his play, different versions of confrontation and survival would come forth, analogous in my mind to pieces of dreams which are important to us and we remember vividly, but that seem to come out of nowhere. In one such session, Jack dramatized the story of a horse who survived deathly experiences repeatedly, each time undergoing healing and in the end getting a special kind of a home made just for him, guaranteeing his protection.

Resurrection was a common variant of survival in Jack's imagination, but about one-third of the way through therapy Jack imagined a birth story, which is very different from rebirth. As he told the story, his language and his demeanor matched the magical unfolding of events, and the resulting product seemed temporarily to transfix him.

> Santa Claus is delivering presents when he receives a call from an elf to report Mrs Claus was in the hospital. Santa returns and when he arrives at the hospital Mrs Claus has died, but Santa thought of a magic potion (using the magic in the stars) to get back her life. A couple years later getting ready for a sleigh ride they "fell, fell, fell" and then woke up to little babies who "grew, grew, grew," and at the end of the story the elves bumped into each other. The moral is, never bump into each other.
>
> But, after the elves did there is a giant sand volcano. They put "layers and layers and layers" on it. They made a hole and put lava in it [Jack pours water into the center] and then it blew and made a little island that is called Baby Santa's Island.

Jack's play typically involved a lot of movement, leaving home, or a post, or delivering a pizza, as examples. In this session, Jack explored movement in new directions. He seemed to be crossing old, invisible boundaries, pioneering through space and deep into the earth. The movements were exponentially more expansive and less constrained. There was falling through space, building up the layers of a volcano, lava positioning itself in a volcano, and finally the volcano's eruption. While Jack pulled magic from start to finish in this session, including Santa's use of the stars to resurrect his wife, birthing babies and the compression of time into a volcano, the final stroke of magic reflects the uniqueness of Jack's voice, which he has birthed through his imagination. The final stroke of magic Jack spontaneously named "Baby Santa's Island."

With this Jack had created a new feeling in the room, in me, and of course most importantly, in himself. How precious, how magical, how powerful to create an island! An island is one of the original creations of nature that allows the human race to survive, develop culture, and thrive. And what might "Baby Santa" imply? Could it be the generative power of giving? Of being a beneficent male who is revered in a society more currently seen as conflictual? Baby Santa suggests such goodwill and hope for the future! Could Jack be imagining himself to have the potential to have a significant, esteemed place in his social environment as a male, even with his physical and health needs?

This session seemed to herald the release of Jack's imagination into new dimensions. The play scenes he created from here on often utilized multiple layers of sand and were more elaborate. Jack began creating movies and movie scenes, in which there were sub-plots involving inevitable manipulations and mishaps resulting in severe injury and death and cover-ups on one level, showmanship was established and well-earned honors were awarded and bestowed as another part of the story, and finding some long-ago hidden and forgotten treasure was revealed to be the ultimate goal. Giving voice to all these expressions, we might imagine, Jack was no longer feeling like a shark trying to fit into a shower stall or like a vulnerable bird who needed the collaboration of his army base to survive.

Jack was pulling his own weight in his everyday life also, but was feeling troubled by the demands of a strict teacher. Jack was bright and intelligent, but he had documented learning challenges and delays deriving from his disease. Although he had an Individual Education Plan (IEP), school was often very frustrating. Some of Jack's last sessions were dedicated to the creation of a large clay boulder, and the staging of the imagined demise of this teacher under the weight of the boulder. This was, of course, embedded within an elaborate production, and resulted in various freedoms.

Life is bigger than us individually, and often more than what we feel we can handle. According to Jack's mother, Jack's teacher was strict but caring, reasonable, and appropriate. As Jack's therapist helping him to cope, I did not try to persuade or reason with him to change his perspective or his attitude about school, or his feelings, thoughts, or fantasies. Jack needed and will continue to need to develop more reliable, accessible, and enlivening sources than even his therapist, his parents, or his medical support community to inspire him, as he faces tremendous developmental and health challenges ahead. The journey to one such source, its discovery, and the source itself may very well be made in the stuff of the imagination.

References

Sandburg, C. (1970) 'Washington Monument by Night,' stanza 4, line 2, in *The Complete Poems of Carl Sandburg*, revised and expanded edition. Orlando, FL: Harcourt.

Chapter 7

Dance/Movement Therapy with Children

Rena Kornblum

The purpose of this chapter is to provide you, the reader, with a glimpse into the use of dance/movement therapy (DMT) as a process of accessing and working with children's inner feelings from a developmental framework, using specific case examples to demonstrate the techniques I use. DMT is, as defined by the American Dance Therapy Association, "the psycho-therapeutic use of movement as a process which furthers the emotional, social, cognitive, and physical integration of the individual" (ADTA 2007). Dance/movement therapists use expressive as well as functional movement in their interactions with clients, helping them to access their creativity. It is based on the premise that how we move and hold our bodies reflects how we feel, and that changes experienced on a movement level enable change on all levels.

Our first sense of ourselves is experienced through our body; messages tell us we are wet, hungry, cold, sleepy, warm, and comfortable. The way we are touched and held also affects our sense of self. Throughout life feelings originate as body sensations. Using the body to explore, deal with, and/or resolve these feelings is a powerful tool.

As children grow, they have to work through different developmental tasks to become healthy individuals, such as learning to bond with a significant adult figure and developing a sense of curiosity and mastery. Sometimes things happen that make it difficult to work through these tasks, and as a result restrict the range of physical expression accessible to the individual. Since children learn kinesthetically (non-verbally), these restrictions can impact cognitive as well as emotional growth.

In my work with children I develop therapeutic goals utilizing a developmental model based primarily on Erik Erikson's psychosocial stages in growth, such as trust *versus* mistrust, autonomy *versus* shame and self-doubt, and initiative *versus* guilt (Erikson 1993). I also use Carl Rogers' work on client-centered therapy (Rogers 2003), meeting children where they are and reflecting that back to them through our movement together. Dance therapists are trained to observe movement and have a common vocabulary, first developed by Rudolf Laban (Newlove and Dalby 2004) to communicate these observations. Utilizing this work, Judith Kestenberg, a child psychiatrist, developed a way to analyze movement through a developmental lens. The scope of this chapter does not allow for detailed descriptions of movement analysis but there are many good references providing more detail (Kestenberg-Amighi *et al.* 1999; Kornblum and Lending Halsten 2006; Moore 2005).

Before I begin presenting on my work with children I would like to share one of my own experiences in DMT, the one that convinced me that I should definitely pursue this field. It was 1975. I was in my mid-twenties, trying to decide in what field I should pursue a Master's degree, when a friend from high school introduced me to the field of DMT. I immediately felt a connection to the profession but I wanted to experience DMT for myself before deciding.

One of my goals coming into my own therapy was to become more spontaneous in my interactions with others. I had grown up with an external observer part. I always thought about what I was going to say and do before I did it, which restricted my interactions with others and impacted the range of experiences I allowed myself to try. I had attempted talking about this issue before but found that I was afraid to let go, feeling that I would lose myself somehow if I did. My dance/movement therapist had me experiment with moving freely in the therapy room (moving with high intensity without planning how or what I was going to do) and then regaining control. Through my movement exploration I realized that I could always find the ground beneath me, I could always center myself, no matter how wildly I moved. I had this moment of realization that my fear was groundless; I really could let go and still maintain or regain my sense of self. Then I realized that being in control was part of my core identity. I felt like I was standing at the edge of a cliff. If I let go of my fear and took the leap, I would no longer be able to predict how other people would see me and interact with me or really know who I was anymore; I would be standing on new ground. Continued movement exploration eventually allowed me to take that leap. As I made this major internal shift I realized that it was the movement, the internal experience in my body, that had enabled me to change. I was now convinced that dance/movement therapy was the field for me.

This initial experience impacted the way I learned and processed the theories and techniques presented in my training as a dance/movement therapist. It allowed me to understand how quickly movement can evoke feelings and how the techniques a dance/movement therapist uses, such as meeting clients where they are, structuring sessions around the material the client presents in the here and now, and utilizing and building on clients' strengths, allow the therapeutic process to happen safely (Levy 2005). My own therapeutic experience and my training, which continues to this day, set the foundation for the style and approaches I have developed in my 30 years of working with children. But it is my interactions with the children and families themselves that actually guide my work.

The open-ended structure

One of the things that I liked about my own therapy experience that I brought into my own style is something I call the open-ended technique. In my own work, this structure occurred when I presented my feelings both verbally and non-verbally and my therapist gave me an idea of how to explore them, such as when she suggested that I explore moving wildly and then gain control. The results of this exploration gave my therapist an idea of what to suggest next. In the open-ended technique there is no lesson plan in mind; I develop what I am going to do in the moment.

Case study: George

George came to his in-school DMT group (consisting of three second-grade boys) at 8am on a Monday morning, having had a weekend full of domestic violence that ended with his father in the hospital. He was extremely agitated, pacing around, unable to listen to anyone else, unable to make eye contact, and this mood affected the other two boys. In response to their overstimulation or hyperarousal, my co-therapist and I put on music with a strong beat (the rhythm served as an organizing structure) and spent the first fifteen minutes moving through space, by jumping, slashing, stomping, in synchrony. (*Synchrony*, moving together in the same intensity, spatial pattern, and/or movement style, provides group cohesion.) In response to the boys' continued high, diffuse energy my co-therapist suggested that they try using some of the centering and grounding techniques we had developed previously by pressing with sustained strength against the wall. Sustained use of strength on one thing (the wall) slowed them down and focused them, while still allowing for the intensity of their feelings to be expressed. The boys then suggested taking turns pulling each other around the room on a cloth, still using strength in the pulling, but now using it to interact with each other in a friendly, nurturing way.

During a brief discussion that followed, the boys expressed the feeling that they did not receive support for their anger at home and that the anger felt like pingpong balls bouncing out of control inside of them. In response to both of these images, the lack of support and the bouncing around wildly, I developed a movement experience using a stretch cloth, a commonly used movement prop, made of spandex and sewed with one seam to make it a circular, stretchy enclosure. Two of the three boys and the two therapists acted as anchors, standing with a wide base of support inside the cloth, with the cloth against our backs. We moved backwards, making the cloth into a diamond shape with one of us at each corner. (The cloth became a metaphor for the body.) One child at a time took a turn, starting in the middle of the diamond and running against the cloth, bouncing away to another place, only to bounce again. The child in the middle, enacting the pingpong ball, could be as wild as he wanted while the anchors stood steady as rocks, supporting the anger. The boys were calm and in control when the group ended, reporting how wonderful it felt to be the anger supported by the group.

The open-ended structure is spontaneous; it requires thinking and feeling in the moment, going with what you are given and framing it.

Safe spaces—therapeutic container

In my own therapy, I had to feel safe, and feel that if I really did lose control, my therapist would be able to help me find myself again. Additionally, I needed to know that no matter how strong my feelings were, my therapist would be able to handle them. This experience, in addition to my training, led me to the concept of providing a safe therapeutic container to hold strong feelings. Providing this container allows clients to feel safe, to experience their boundaries being respected, and to develop a sense of trust in their therapist and therapeutic process. In my work with children this process sometimes starts literally, by building safe spaces in the therapy room. Sometimes this space is indicated by a pillow on the floor, sometimes it is indicated by crepe paper set around a person in the size and shape that feels best for him or her, and sometimes it is an area built and decorated with props. It is important that each person's space is considered sacred, not to be entered without permission.

Case study

During the third session of an in-school DMT group for five-to-seven-year-old boys who had witnessed or experienced physical violence, one of the boys, Nathan, shared that his father had sexually abused him over the weekend and that the police had interviewed him. Three things happened after Nathan's sharing. First, many of the other boys began sharing confidential material about drug use and violence in their homes. Second, the rule around confidentiality was re-established; each child promised, while making clear, direct eye contact with me, that they would keep everything said in the group private. I also reminded them that part of my job in keeping them safe was to talk to other adults who could help if I felt they were in danger. And last, everyone expressed agitation and overstimulation via physical restlessness, spatial intrusion, nervous laughter, and needing to move about the room.

I decided that this was an important time to establish a sense of safety to help contain the strong feeling that had emerged, and suggested that each child create a space for himself. The group met in a room that had several small tables, so that each child could make a house defined by the boundaries of a table and then decorate it and make it comfortable using other props such as pillows and brightly colored scarves. There was a distinct change in the mood of the room as each boy became busy building, creating a space that felt comfortable and safe. They were also observant and helpful to others in the group who were struggling to make their "homes" look the way they wanted them to.

After the "homes" were built, therapists and children took turns visiting the different spaces. No one could enter a space without obtaining permission first. This rule established a sense of empowerment and safety for the children. Each boy, who outside the therapy room was impulsive, intrusive, and often out of control, was very careful to follow this rule. It seemed important, in light of all the material they had shared, that safety and boundaries be respected.

The boys were enthralled with their creations. At this point, I took out paper and markers and asked each child to draw a picture of what a safe space was like for him. They could decide if there were locks on doors, if doors were open or closed, what was in the space, what surrounded the space, etc. Art work here served as another non-verbal mode of communication, integrating the body experience of building a space, which was limited to the space and props available, with a graphic experience in which they could draw whatever they wanted. One child had barbed wire around his space. One child had a climbing structure in his space to move around on as much as he wanted to.

This session marked a change in the arousal level in the group. Each session began with the children finding a spot in the room that they could go to if they felt overwhelmed or scared. We began to use these safe spaces as nests to be contained safely in and to move from, out into the world.

Developmentally, abuse triggers issues in the earliest stage of development, trust *versus* mistrust (Erikson 1993). The work of creating safe spaces directly addressed this issue by making the therapy room a safe place, re-establishing a sense of trust, and demonstrating that the boys' strong feelings would be respected and contained.

Meeting a child where s/he is

When I started therapy, my therapist began with the material I brought to the session. I was very nervous to begin with, and she moved with me, starting with the nervous energy and gradually bringing in some calming movement. The fact that she met me right where I was gave me the feeling of being seen, heard, and accepted. Dance/movement therapists frequently do this by moving with their clients, sometimes actually mirroring them, sometimes matching their energy using voice and/or movement. This is how healthy parents attune with their children and how attachment develops.

Case study: Will

Will was a five-year-old boy who had been sexually abused by a babysitter at the age of two. His mother and school staff were worried because he showed disassociative tendencies—looking blank, not responding when asked to do anything in front of his class or at a large gathering, and being non-compliant and angry. Will's mother, who had been physically and emotionally abused as a child, was now afraid of abusing her son and wanted family therapy to work on their issues.

The day of our first session Will appeared angry and did not want to come to the therapy room. I accepted that feeling and we sat silently together for a few minutes, and then played with some toys in the waiting area. I did not challenge Will's resistance; I stayed with it and gave him some time to get used to me (being with him where he was without getting upset). Within five minutes he willingly came with his mother to the therapy room, where he became quite excited. He began running around and setting up jumping challenges for himself. His mother became very anxious that he would hurt himself and kept trying to get him to stop. As I observed Will I noticed that he had two types of energy, one that was in control, when he could jump and balance without hurting himself, and one that was out of control, during which he fell and ran into the wall.

I commented on these two distinct states and Will decided to name them, calling the part of himself that was in control the "super cheetah" and the part that was out of control the "mountain lion." I started out by having his mom move with Will and me, mirroring his movement as he showed us how the two parts felt inside. This technique is called "attuning to" or "matching" someone, and it increases the feeling of being seen and accepted for who you are.

Will's mom identified with the idea of these two parts and decided to name her own out-of-control, angry part the "wild stallion" and her in-control part the "super goat." Will loved that his mother could connect with him on this level and he started enacting a series of adventures with his mother and me. These involved switching between his two animal parts while his mom and I were directed to try to catch and control him. These stories always involved the themes of chasing and staying free, indicating Will's need for autonomy and power, Erikson's second stage of development. Again, I accepted Will where he was and went with the material he brought to the session.

The concept of identifying which part was in charge became something this family began using at home to help them diffuse anger. They agreed that any time the out-of-control part was in charge or seemed to be trying to take over, either of them could cue the other one to take a break and breathe or go to their own room until the in-control part was back in charge. This may sound like splitting a client's personality instead of working toward integration, but integration comes with an understanding that we all have many facets to our personality and that each contributes something to the whole. I call this technique "part selves" and I developed it by integrating the needs of children to express feelings in movement with the concept (from Gestalt therapy (Perls 1980) and voice dialogue therapy) of parts of the self dialoguing or interacting with other parts (Stone and Stone 1988). The "part selves" technique gave this family a non-judgmental way to describe behavior, allowing for the idea that they could change.

Developmentally appropriate/functional movement: a psycho-educational approach

Sometimes children are not ready to work on deep psychological issues. Before they are ready to let go of old behaviors they may need to enlarge their movement repertoire, building on strengths or developing new inner and interactional behaviors. I think, in a way, this also happened to me. Although I realized that I could regain control whenever I needed to, I wasn't ready to take the leap to a new place (change my way of interacting) before building my skills in the therapy session.

Case study

A group of seven boys from kindergarten were very difficult to handle in school. They were very excitable and distractible. The first several months of DMT sessions were spent on giving them experiences in modulating their energy. I started with their preferred mode of moving, high energy, by introducing high energy that was in control. Each child, individually at first and then in pairs and trios, was given a count of twenty in which to move energetically without touching anyone or anything in the room (other than the floor) and to be able to stop without falling when the count was finished. We then practiced moving in low energy, in slow motion, for example, modulating the energy between high and low, then setting up environments in the room and moving through them in different energies. After the boys gained more control over their bodies we were able to develop therapeutic stories that introduced emotional themes.

Sometimes the skills that are introduced are emotionally based, feeling charades, for example, or playful enactment of strong feelings such as anger. Many of the children I see have anger issues due either to violence and abuse in their environment, or to other types of trauma such as removal from the family or illness, or simply because of temperament or developmental struggles. Both the children and the adults in their lives frequently see this anger as a negative emotion. One thing that often surprises children in DMT is that their anger is welcomed as a helpful voice to tell them what they need and when that need is not getting met. The skill that is introduced in response to this strong feeling is knowing how to be angry safely.

Case study: Raymond

A five-year-old boy named Raymond frequently lost control at school and at home whenever something did not go his way. He had to be removed from class several times a day for kicking, throwing, hitting, etc. He tended to escalate from disappointment to rage within seconds. In the initial session of a group of four five-year-old children, Raymond was enjoying a movement experience. When it was time to end and sit back down on our pillows (used as safe, grounding place markers), I could see that he was getting angry. I quickly went over to him and said, "I am so glad that you are showing us how you feel. I can see that you are angry. Does anyone in this group know some safe ways to show anger?" Raymond and the other children looked up in surprise. They had never heard anyone express pleasure at anger before. After brainstorming about ways to be mad safely, the whole group stood up and began stomping around the movement space while shouting "NO!" at the top of their lungs. The idea of having fun with their anger was totally intriguing. We ended the session by experimenting with ways to calm down before going back to class. Interestingly enough, Raymond was the only child who could actually express modulation from angry to happy in his body. For the next two weeks, every time Raymond saw me in the hallway at school he excitedly asked about coming back to the group and having time to express his anger.

In this group, emotions were actively expressed, and skills such as how to be mad safely and how to self-settle from strong emotions were incorporated at the same time.

Structured *versus* improvisational movement

My own therapy consisted of a lot of movement exploration in which I was given a theme to improvise to movement. After I moved, my therapist and I would verbally process the feelings and themes that emerged. Sometimes my sessions with children involve structured exploration, as in the two examples given above (using a psycho-educational approach), but sometimes children are able to improvise and use that in much the same way I did—to open up issues and make them approachable.

Case study: Samantha

Samantha was a seven-year-old child whose crack-addicted mother abandoned her in another state. She had been exposed to many traumatic situations before her recent move to her father's house. At school Samantha would have lengthy tantrums, requiring four adults to carry her out of the classroom. Once upset she would stay upset for the rest of the day. According to her teachers and her father, she never spoke about her mother. Samantha was placed in an in-school DMT therapy group with four other second-grade girls dealing with trauma. The children liked to make up dances for the group to watch.

"Being seen," which connects to Carl Rogers' theory of "being heard" (Rogers 2003), is one of the most important therapeutic goals for individuals dealing with trauma. The children loved the fact that four other children, my co-therapist, and myself were witnessing their dances. From the beginning of the group, all of Samantha's dances were about loss. She identified herself as an orphaned baby cheetah that had to take care of herself. One day she lay down on the floor on one side of the room and attempted to reach the other side. She used her hands and legs to drag herself, but no matter how hard she tried to get there, which you could see by the strength and tension in her body, she could not make progress. (This movement behavior is related to the earliest stage of Erikson's psychosocial development, trust *versus* mistrust, and the helpless, hopeless feelings that develop when the child's earliest needs are not met (Erikson 1993).) Samantha pretended to cry, calling for her mother, but the extreme effort she made resulted in her being frozen in place. The group sat, spellbound by her dance, by the expression of her longing. Then some of the girls offered to help her, to pull her, but she shook her head "no." The dance represented the inability to reach her goal; she somehow understood that all the pulling and support would not fulfill her sense of emptiness.

However, the act of expressing the unspeakable and having that witnessed and felt by the others in the group enabled Samantha to make significant changes. Within a month or two of her joining the group, her teachers reported that she could now settle and have a positive day after a tantrum. Within three months her tantrums had decreased in frequency and intensity and she no longer needed to be carried out of her class. In the group she occasionally began to make dances and movement stories with other children. Some of these dances actually showed joy and lightness, several showed connection to others, and friendships were developing (something she had never experienced before).

Felt experience followed by symbolic expression

While using non-verbal methods of communication to work on expressing the unspeakable and creating a sense of wholeness, I like to have a connection from the felt experience to the symbolic. I think this is particularly helpful with children, since they both live more naturally in their bodies than adults and are less articulate. The vast majority of the children I work with are referred to therapy because of acting out or withdrawn behavior. Most of them are not facile at verbalizing their feelings but are able to make verbal connections after we have a moving experience.

Case study: Jason

Jason was a young child dealing with autism. He used echolalia for most of his speech, and would scream endlessly at different sound frequencies, such as sirens and the public television channel. Our session frequently consisted of moving together in ways that Jason would initiate and I would structure. For example, we would make up conversations on the drum. Jason would play and I would respond. Jason liked music a lot and was able to use songs to express his feelings. While frustrated during speech testing one day, for example, he broke into the song *It's a Hard Day's Night*. I like to improvise musically and I found that anytime Jason was having a hard time in school or at home, if I could make sense of it through our movement and then sing about it, Jason's problematic behavior would stop.

I feel that Jason and many children need to be seen and understood. Moving together is one way of doing this; drawing, singing, and talking are ways of augmenting the movement.

Developmental perspective

In order to synthesize the concepts presented above and show how the combination of a developmental perspective and movement observation allow me to assess my clients, I will present a slightly longer case example. This example also demonstrates that whatever feelings and conflicts are present and whatever goals I set from my analysis, when I go into the therapy room with a client, I am interacting with a person in the here and now.

In addition to the synthesis of techniques already presented, I will also introduce the use of humor, which can create an environment where self-expression can take place. Humor, as explained by Freud, is a technique of working through resistances and gaining mastery of a conflictual area (Bernet 1993). I use humor by exaggerating some of the clients' issues in my body. My clients are often able to laugh at a defense or an interactional pattern they commonly use when they see it reflected this way, and so this becomes the first step in making a change.

Case study: Amelia

Amelia was a 16-year-old girl on the autistic spectrum, whose alcoholic mother had died. She now lived with a strict, severe grandmother who did not show any warmth to her granddaughter. Amelia made minimal eye contact, held her head either down or turned to the right, and thrust her chest forward and her pelvis back. She had extreme amounts of tension throughout her body, which made all her movements appear disjointed; they did not flow through her body. When Amelia did move, the movements were generally small and close to her body. She showed an exaggerated startle response to any noise louder than a speaking voice. Amelia held herself as still as possible, as if she would like to be invisible. Despite this withdrawal, Amelia showed evidence of potential and a desire to break through the fear. She showed a wider movement repertoire in our intake session, with a small smile as she interacted with me. She also showed evidence of feelings and conflicts beneath the surface, for example, her facial grimaces indicating anger.

Movement analysis indicated that Amelia was still dealing with early developmental issues. With this in mind I developed a set of therapeutic goals:

- develop a trusting relationship with the therapist and extend that trust to others in her world

- increase eye contact

- increase body awareness and decrease extreme body tension

- enlarge movement repertoire, developing more flexible use of all movement qualities

- increase gross motor coordination

- develop social skills

- increase self-esteem

- increase verbal skills.

I saw Amelia twice a week for 45-minute DMT sessions. She liked movements done on the floor, such as rolling along a mat or rolling a ball back and forth. We were able to create games about moving towards and away from each other. Amelia also liked sensory stimulation, such as pressing nerf balls (soft balls made of foam) against her body and having me do the same thing. There were little giggles when I would move with her, and an increase in fleeting eye contact. These movements indicated a very low level of development, reinforcing my initial assessment.

After a month of following her lead, I began to introduce some additional activities such as Jacobson progressive relaxation (Jacobson 1974). We ended each session lying on the floor, tensing and releasing different muscle groups. Amelia liked having me try to swing her arms to see if she was relaxed. We also began to dance to music that Amelia chose. During the dancing Amelia would use frequent but fleeting eye contact with a sideways glance. She would rock from side to side and occasionally travel past me during the dance.

As a new therapist, I became anxious for a change after a few months. I tried to introduce new movement ideas that were at a higher level. Amelia, who was not yet at that level, ignored my ideas and continued with rolling towards and away, pressing foam balls, and doing simple dancing movements. I slowed myself down and reminded myself of the phrase I had often heard during my training: "Follow the movement process, the movement will take you where you need to go." This became my mantra as I worked to accept Amelia and follow her lead. For the first year of therapy we worked on developing a relationship and integrating and relaxing her body.

The session I am about to describe took place in the beginning of our second year together. The session began with a warm-up. Amelia selected and put on the music, saying loudly, "Me can do it myself now." The warm-up emphasized rhythm and grounding as we established body and visual rapport. I asked Amelia where she was tense, and she indicated her shoulders. We worked on relaxing them and activating ourselves.

I had been told that Amelia was making more eye contact in her classroom and was beginning to relate more to her peers. I asked her if she could tell me some of the changes she had experienced in the past year. She immediately withdrew, her eyes went down and her torso retreated. She said that nothing had changed, that she was still afraid of everything and did not want to become brave or to change in any way. At first I pushed her to talk about how she had changed, despite her fear. Of course, pushing a client when they are not ready does not work.

I then asked Amelia to show me what she did with her body when she was scared. I mirrored her, exaggerating her fear, and moved with her briefly. We then looked in the mirror and I had Amelia describe herself. I teasingly said that if she wanted to stay scared, that's what we would do. We walked around the room for five minutes with no eye contact and extreme body tension. Amelia then said she was tired and wanted to stop. I pushed her to continue, saying that I thought she wanted to stay scared. Amelia liked humor and the teasing was done in a respectful manner.

Instinctively I felt that Amelia was ready for a change. She was already transferring some of our work into the classroom and was verbalizing pride in her ability to use the stereo independently. So instead of backing down when Amelia showed resistance, I made a therapeutic intervention and asked her if she could show me how she would stand and move if she were brave. There was a startling change in her body attitude. Amelia faced me directly with hands on hips and a wide base of support. I again mirrored her and asked her to move. Following her lead, we stayed in place, stomping our feet, making slashing and punching movements downward and away from our bodies. At first the rhythm was disjointed but I verbally emphasized the downbeat, and for one of the first times, Amelia's movements appeared rhythmic and connected. She spontaneously shouted, "Not scared of anything!" We again looked in the mirror and Amelia described her body and what was different.

We made a game of alternating, at Amelia's command, between the "scared" and "brave" body attitudes described above. We started on opposite sides of the room and walked past each other, either making no eye contact and mumbling to ourselves, or looking directly at each other, shouting, "I'm not scared of anything," stamping and punching.

We ended with a few moments of centering quiet movements, turned off the music and did relaxation, with Amelia lying on the floor. We went through the progression of tensing and relaxing isolated body parts while concentrating on the breathing that we did each session.

There were several interventions that helped make this session successful:

- mirroring—following Amelia's movement when she expressed fear of change

- humor—playfully teasing her to help her work through her resistance

- open-ended structure—when the moment was right, I requested something new.

If Amelia had not been ready for the change she would have ignored my request, and I would have accepted her and her feelings.

Summary

This chapter has presented ideas and techniques related to the use of DMT with children, including:

- the use of an open-ended structure—going with what you, the therapist, are given in the moment and framing it, which encourages spontaneity and requires the therapist to think on his/her feet

- the importance of meeting a child where s/he is through mirroring, matching movement qualities, and witnessing, which creates a feeling of attunement with a client

- the concept of the therapy space as a safe container for strong feelings—respecting, being with, and matching all the emotional parts of the client. This can include physically building a safe space

- the relevance of going from the felt experience, through movement, to the symbolic expression of the experience through verbalization, drawing, and/or singing

- a way of using a developmental and observational framework to analyze and set goals for a client, and how that analysis translates into the therapy experience.

There are many more approaches and concepts involved in DMT with children. I hope that those presented here have been helpful in giving you a deeper understanding of the non-verbal work done in the field of Dance/Movement Therapy.

References

American Dance Therapy Association (2007) Accessed 9 September, 2007 at: http://www.adta.org/about/factsheet.cfm.

Bernet, W. (1993) 'Humor in evaluating and treating children and adolescents.' *Journal of Psychotherapy Practice and Research 2*, 307–317. Palo Alto, CA: American Psychiatric Press, Inc.

Erikson, E. (1993) *Childhood and Society.* New York, NY: W.W. Norton and Co.

Jacobson, E. (1974) *Progressive Relaxation: A Physiological and Clinical Investigation of Muscular States and their Significance in Psychology and Medical Practice.* Denton, TX: University of Chicago Press.

Kestenberg-Amighi, J., Loman, S., Lewis, P. and Sossin, K.M. (1999) *The Meaning of Movement: Developmental and Clinical Perspectives of the Kestenberg Movement Profile.* Amsterdam: Gordon and Breach Publishers.

Kornblum, R. and Lending Halsten, R. (2006) 'In-school dance/movement therapy for traumatized children.' In S. Brooke (ed.) *Creative Arts Therapy Manual.* Springfield, IL: Charles C. Thomas.

Levy, F. (2005) *Dance/Movement Therapy: A Healing Art.* Reston, VA: National Dance Association.

Moore, C. (2005) *Movement and Making Decisions: The Body–Mind Connection in the Workplace.* New York, NY: Dance and Movement Press.

Newlove, J. and Dalby, J. (2004) *Laban for All.* New York, NY: Routledge: Taylor and Francis Group.

Perls, F. (1980) *The Gestalt Approach and Eye-Witness to Therapy.* London: Bantam Press Publishers.

Rogers, C.R. (2003) *Client-centered Therapy.* London: Constable and Robinson Publishers.

Stone, H. and Stone, S. (1998) *Embracing Ourselves: The Voice Dialogue Manual.* Novato, CA: New World Library.

Chapter 8

The Healing Power of Creative Expression

Nancy Mangano Rowe

I walk into my therapy room. It feels empty. I begin to rearrange the room and mentally greet the sand, prepare the room… I set the intention for healing to take place in the room. I close my eyes by the sand tray, open and take a deep long breath, releasing the outer world…sinking into a moment of meditation, centering. As I open my eyes, I notice which miniature speaks to me today. Which figure seems to resonate with my psyche on this day. I notice that the giraffe seems to have more energy than the other miniatures today. I place it in the sand and take it in! I project onto it…with as few words as possible; I begin to wonder what the giraffe is saying to me. In what ways will I have to stick my neck out today? In what ways might I need to take a risk? I sense that inner knowing. I hear the door to the waitingroom open. My first client has arrived. I look back at my room and feel into my body. The energy field has deepened. I am ready for my day.

Introduction

I am an expressive arts therapist who uses sandplay, play therapy, and expressive arts therapy when working with young children. The images and sand scenes that children create during a session have always fascinated me. Even more fascinating are the repetitive patterns of images that seem to morph and transform over the weeks and months as children find ways to face difficult life events. Years ago, I read an article about a young child who worked through her grief over her dad's death by writing a story. She wrote, revised, and shared this very short story for close to a year. Then, one day, she announced that her story was finished. At this time, it was clear to the therapist that she had reached a significant stage of recovery from her grief. I have noticed similar types of non-verbal stories and narratives play out over long periods of time. The same figures and similar motifs emerge in sand scenes. Each time it happens, something changes, something new is born, something else is revealed, very much like in the story about Daddy dying. It is often only after a sequence of activity, a series of expressions, or months of making sand scenes, that we can fully appreciate the healing that has taken place in the context of the therapeutic setting.

This chapter explores what I refer to as "movement of transformation" as it is revealed through sandplay, play therapy, and the expressive art process. I will discuss the therapeutic relationship during non-verbal, symbolic play, and the importance of creating a "free and protected" space for healing to emerge. Examples that illustrate transformative movements over time will be shared. In order to protect my clients, I have used composite examples and changed names. In this chapter, I ask the question, where is the juice in non-verbal therapeutic process? What are the conditions from which this healing process can emerge?

Healing through applied imagination

My training as a counselor has been diverse, including marriage and family therapy, expressive arts therapy, play therapy, psychosynthesis, authentic movement, and counseling. Each of these fields holds a variety of theoretical frames. It is important to state my personal beliefs and assumptions.

Assumption 1: most people have a natural impulse to move toward greater wholeness

Jeremy Taylor (2007) in his dream workshops that our dreams, sleeping or waking, are always in the service of wholeness. The expressive arts and the play therapy process are waking dreams. I believe that most humans wish to be more whole and that this is their natural impulse (Kalff 1991; Levine 1999; Rogers 1990; Rogers 1999). We are on a journey of individuation, the process of becoming conscious of human wholeness and moving toward integration (Kalff 1991).

In his book *If You Turned into a Monster* Dennis McCarthy describes the individuation process, attributed to Carl Jung, as a self-actualization process.

He says, "It is a journey we begin from the moment we are born and it is possible to look at all dreams, all creative imaginings, that occur, especially within the context of therapy, as the efforts of our deeper self to help us actualize this journey, as well as an expression of the enormous resistance most of us have to it" (2007, p.29).

Assumption 2: the expressive arts and symbolic play can activate the energies that facilitate the individuation process

Imagination and symbolic play through sandplay, play therapy, and expressive arts therapy within the context of the therapy room create the conditions where healing is possible. Imagination helps children to discover what is hidden in their life and to shape their relationship to the world, which they are constantly constructing and co-constructing. It gives them access to that which they cannot express verbally and helps them to move more fluidly through life circumstances (Levine 1999).

Dennis McCarthy feels that symbols we produce through applied imagination in the context of the therapeutic setting are ways of fitting in and belonging "to both our deeper and higher selves and to the greater human tribe and even to the cosmos" (2007, p.29). The symbols that children use reflect parts of themselves that are deep and often beyond words. "When a child makes a drawing, tells a story, or makes a scene in the sandbox, we have before us in symbolic form the closest glimpse possible of the human psyche. They not only become what they create; they are this with no clear delineation" (2007, p.30). McCarthy, like art therapist/educator Shaun McNiff (1992), believes that use of imagination is akin to ancient shamanic practices, and that here too the client works with archetypal forms and myths in the healing process. When in the presence of a sand scene, McCarthy explains, the child's psyche is actually to some extent "in the sand." This is especially so when the play is charged, that is, when there is a palpable sense of aliveness in the play configuration. In these numinous moments there is no separation between the child and their imaginings. Body and psyche are one and equally present in the activity (McCarthy 2007, p.30). Like myths, the sandplay process becomes a spontaneous expression of the psyche at a particular moment in time and space (Markell 2002). Body and psyche are one and equally present in the activity. As a result of the embodied experience of the sandplay process, during charged moments remarkable transformation is possible (Markell 2002; McCarthy 2007).

This is true within all therapeutic forms of creative expression and play therapy. At some non-verbal level, symbolic play invites the client to better understand life circumstances and to transform, re-integrate, and renew themselves. They are better able to discover, integrate, and transcend inner polarities and to accept their disowned and shadow parts, reach deeper self-acceptance, and move toward their wholeness. As Natalie Rogers explains, "As we journey inward to discover our essence or wholeness, we discover our relatedness to the outer world. The inner and outer world become one" (1999, p.131).

Assumption 3: playing and the creative process is in its self-healing

Expressive arts therapists are well aware of the healing power of the creative process, even outside of the therapy room. They generally agree that while the image that emerges from creative expression provides important information and gives clients insights into their psyche, it is really the process of creation that is transformative (Levine 1999; McNiff 1992; Rogers 1999).

> Our sense of the creative process moves beyond the self-referential world of the person of the artist. We are interested in the things that come to us, move through us, and influence us. The making of a painting is an expression for that aspect of the psyche that changes, transforms, and constantly creates new life. The psyche is itself restructured in response to the influences of its own creation. (McNiff 1992, p.65)

Paolo Knill considers the expressive arts to be "rituals of play" and believes that painting, acting, dancing, music-making, storytelling, and all forms of the expressive arts provide the vessel, the safe container, for people to heal and visit "existential themes, pathos and mystery." "The arts…provide the multiplicity and opportunity to explore the unthinkable, a space beyond morality, a traditional playground of light and shadow" (Knill 1999, p.45).

Assumption 4: the creative process is an intermodal activity and establishing a creative connection can deepen the therapeutic experience

Inherent in the art process is the natural way that all perceptions and senses are used during the creative process. It is, by its very nature, an intermodal process. In other words, we hear and see and feel a stream of experience. We naturally use our bodies as we use our senses in the experience of painting.

When we use the creative arts and imaginative play in a therapeutic setting, it is quite natural to bring in all of our senses. To separate an expressive movement from an image or to isolate a drawing as part of a therapeutic process may short cut the deeper levels of the creative process, which in itself is healing.

Natalie Rogers recognizes the importance of the interplay between various creative forms that clients use in therapy, and has introduced the conscious use of interplay among the various expressive arts forms: movement, art, writing, and sound. She calls this *the creative connection.* By encouraging the creative connection, clients can more fully embody their emotional energy and deepen their experience and healing potential. She explains that through the creative connection, we awaken to new possibilities and inner transformation. In creative connection the therapist bridges one art form to another intentionally, which heightens and intensifies the inward journey (Rogers 1997). By moving from one art modality to another, we release layers of material and come to our center, where we can more fully access our creative potential.

When a client is given the opportunity to move the story and the image in a process where more than one of the senses is used, or from one form to another, a deepening occurs and the client is able to understand their experience through a variety of lenses and give voice to that experience. The following examples demonstrate how the creative connection might work.

Case study: the dance

One nine-year-old girl, Sue, who felt a lot of anger, spent much time exploring her feeling through expressive arts and play. During one session, toward the end of her therapy process, she used pastels to create a series of images that reflected her journey through the anger. She carefully placed these images over the floor of the therapy room. She ordered and re-ordered them until she was satisfied. She then began to *dance* the images. As she moved from image to image, she embodied the feeling within each image. This process supported her therapy process and helped to empower her movement toward resolving some of the issues related to her anger.

Case study: the language of the creative arts and sandplay

Amy, a nine-year-old child, lived in an unstable home situation. Her mother had a habitual pattern of leaving relationships, and would sometimes become abusive with her partner in front of Amy. In the early stages of the therapy, Amy created a large mound in the middle of the sand scene, with activity around the outside of the mound. Close to the mound were three firefighters.

During the early stages of Amy's therapy, her mother had found a new partner, moved in with him, and found a new job working with this person. Amy began to show signs of optimism. Each week, she would come into the therapy room and create a sand tray with a mound in the center. I watched as she took several firefighters and slowly, week by week, deconstructed the mound. It got smaller and less solid over time.

Then one day, her mother shared that she had become physically violent with her boyfriend. The stability of the home situation began to crumble. It became clear that the mother would soon be moving on. I sensed that this would be my last time seeing this young child. This became more and more clear as the child asked me to work with her in the sandplay. We sat side by side as she guided my hands. She made two large mounds and put my hands on one of them. She then began to make her own mound harder and higher, and packed it down really hard. She moved my hands so that I would do the same—then looked at me as I sensed the hardness of the shell around the mound. I sensed that she was showing me that she needed to protect herself from what was to come in her life.

The two mounds stayed put in the sandtray. No firefighters were there to deconstruct them. Instead, Amy began to pat the sand down to make it harder and harder. She left that afternoon, and I never saw her again. I found out later that Amy and her mother had once again left town.

What was it that gave Amy the feeling that she was safe in the therapy, that despite her unstable home life she could share so fully through her expressive play? I address this question in the following pages.

Temenos: creating free and protected space

Play therapists and expressive arts therapists create a sense of safety through their relationship to the child and in the unique environment of the play therapy room. They create, in a sense, a sanctuary where healing energies can emerge. I parallel this to entering a dojo in the practice of Aikido, a Japanese martial art form that cultivates harmonious and healthy living through the practice of its form. When aikido students enter a dojo, or training area, they bow to the physical space to honor the self-cultivation that is about to occur in this container. All activity that happens in this space is considered "sacred." Likewise, the child enters the play therapy room to participate in a ritual of sorts that invites a psychospiritual narrative to be expressed, allowing some part of the child to be opened, stirred, shifted, or in some way transformed. This special type of holding environment, be it the Aikido dojo or the play therapy space, is called temenos. This comes from the Greek word meaning a piece of land dedicated for sacred purposes. Others may think of it as the therapeutic holding environment, or use some other name. By whatever name it is known, there is a degree of unpredictability and mystery (Mandelbaum 2006) that helps the client to enter into an organic, spontaneous process that comes from a deep and usually non-verbal place, a place that is often created and contained in relative silence while the play or expression is in process. This silence allows both the client and the therapist to hear and respond to the *voice of the soul* (Signell 1996).

Sandplay and creative arts therapists' transformational work can only occur if the therapist creates a safe place for this work to happen. Clients arrive at the sand tray, the art paper, and the therapy room to complete a healing process. They enter into this "free and protected space" and recognize it as a "fertile, energetic field" (Mandelbaum 2006, p.116). When the session is complete, the client leaves the room changed, or has shifted in some way.

During the art-making or sandplay process, clients have the opportunity to project their internal processes, their pain, sorrows, hopes, dreams, anything that may arrive through our imagination, into a form through which they can begin to transform it in their outer lives (Kalff 1991; Mandelbaum 2006; Markell 2002). Here the client can transform shadow material and destructive tendencies into integration and wholeness. It is the therapist's task to cultivate *temenos*, a place where the client feels free to explore without interruption or judgment.

When Amy was able to deconstruct the mound in the sand tray over time, she was able, with the help of the miniature firefighters, to tame her own inner fire and bring more of herself into her daily life. When she began to see that her home situation was about to unravel again, she symbolically constructed a shell that protected her and allowed her to contain this energy. In the therapy room, in the presence of the therapist who had created a solid, trusting relationship with her, and with the archetypal firefighter miniatures, she was able to enter into a process that supported her healing.

Metzner (1986) likens the effect of transformation to a forest fire that transforms the landscape.

> After a fire, the landscape is the same, but the character is somewhat unrecognizable. Soon the land is bursting again with new growth. It has been restructured. Transformation impacts our core and dissolves barriers so that actual structures and functioning of the psyche are changed. In the healing process transformation is seen by how a

person's life is changed, by the person's desire to participate in the outer world. (Clements 2003)

By working through imagination and symbol, whether the imaginative process is a visual, auditory, or kinesthetic process, we begin to experience the transformation of psychic energy. This happens because "symbols are *energy laden*" (McCarthy 2007). Over time, this energy can profoundly change the internal psychological complexes that result in changes in the external world as well. In children, we see this happen by the way that they change their relationship to their family, in a reduction of physical symptoms, or in changes in their social relationship in school or at home (McCarthy 2007).

Healing in the sand

Sandplay, when used without a specified purpose, creates conditions for transformation to occur. It has been described as a pilgrimage (Markell 2002; Ryce-Menuhin 1992), a journey toward renewal and healing. Sandplay provides the fertile ground that evokes archetypal energies. In the sand children encounter through symbolic play, conditions where psychologically necessary experiences that may be dark and destructive well up and may as a result be transformed (Ryce-Menuhin 1992). Myths or universal stories that are played out in sandplay provide archetypal forms, which in turn access energy that allows for personal integration and transformation (Markell 2002; Singer 1994).

June Singer (1994) explains that archetypes are pre-formed patterns of thinking or being in this world and include motifs or primordial images. Archetypes represent regular and consistently recurring types of situations and types of figures. These current patterns might include motifs like *the hero's quest* or archetypal images like *the divine child*, or *the trickster, the wise woman* or *the primordial mother*.

As Karen Signell (1996, p.75) so beautifully explains, children "discover, through their brave movements in the sand, how to confront their world as it really seems deep inside them, in its own language. They find how to change it or inwardly come to terms with it. They move their inner furniture—the objects. When they shift the sand, they shift their psychic topography and the very basis of their being, to follow the deeper currents of their life."

This personal journey of transformation can only be experienced across time, over many sessions, as children play out their own myths. The therapist notices each sand scene, and also notices how each child responds as he or she enters into the experience of the fully embodied, fully lived story that facilitates the healing impulse. As we watch and witness children over time, we observe how they come to terms with life circumstances and mature.

Noticing the journey of transformation

> For us to be present to them is to appreciate their struggle and let ourselves be moved by terrible things and touched by awe and beauty. That is enough. It is not necessary to have diagnostic words to name or categorize this kind of process. People naturally know how to forage, and we know how to be shepherds. (Signell 1996, p.76)

In this section, I will highlight several examples of transformative movements that I have noticed in working with children. This is not an attempt to categorize or classify, but rather to open the conversation to the notion that as therapists we can observe this movement without interfering with the process of transformation.

The monster picture

"The monster picture" is an activity described in Dennis McCarthy's book, *If You Turned into a Monster* (2007). The directions are simple. The therapist asks the child to draw him- or herself as a monster. McCarthy says it can give access to the vital expression of energy in children in a non-verbal, visceral way. He describes it as an act filled with instinct and emotions, one that points the way toward healing. It helps the therapist to feel into the child's experiences and feelings in the moment.

When I ask a child to draw him- or herself as a monster, I am interested in the feeling of the monster and where the energy or lack of it shows in the monstrous form. If this is not the first monster the child has drawn I notice how the form and energy has shifted. In a sense the monster is both an expressive experience and an assessment technique that demonstrates what progress is being made. I use the form and the child's drawing of it to inform me as to what else might be needed for them to feel stronger, freer, or more able to discharge negativity.

Case study: the mermaid

Gwen, a heavy-set ten-year-old, walks into the therapy room alongside her very petite mother. She is dressed very neatly in her jeans and feminine shirt; her hair is pushed back with barrettes. I ask her to draw what she would look like if she turned into a monster, a drawing that I use to explore where a child is in the moment. Gwen has drawn her inner monster twice previously. I give her many choices of art materials. She chooses pastels, one of the more messy options. For a moment I find myself disconnected from being present as I ask her if she wants tissues so that she can keep her hands clean. By this time, I hear her breath deepen and feel the quality of the room shift. I have learned to pay attention when I hear this particular visceral response. I have come to understand this quality of breathing as a deepening process. She says "no" to the tissues and is intently focussed on drawing her mermaid. She doesn't look at it until it is completed. The mermaid is beautiful, with long, blond, flowing hair, a smile, and big eyes. I am imagining that the monster drawing is complete, but then without speaking Gwen puts her palm in the middle of the mermaid and smears it and then rubs the chalk onto her clean jeans. She looks and says, "Now I am done."

Commentary

I am aware of the paradox that exists as I witness this young girl. I notice how particularly well groomed she is today and how she chose the messiest drawing material that was offered to her. I am aware of my discomfort when she chooses the pastels and how I want to take care of her "messiness." I am also aware how this caretaking takes me away from the therapeutic moment. I notice the contrast between her and her mom's body types as they walk in today and her mom's face when she walks out the door with pastels on her daughter's formerly spotless jeans. I notice the perfect little mermaid drawn when I asked Gwen to draw the monster. But, most important, I felt the energy in the room deepen quickly and with intensity, and even more so when she took the chalk drawing and smeared it. I notice the intensity subside when she declares: "I'm done." Gwen's perfect mermaid was smeared with such intensity I asked myself how to further help her to express this messiness, to loosen up, open up, and drop the illusion of perfection.

Transformation through repetition

I am often amazed at how the same images, miniatures, sounds, stories, and movement are repeated over time during expressive therapy sessions. Repetition is central to the process of working through difficult issues and events in expressive arts and play therapy. It is a natural part of life's process. You can see this same repetitive pattern when children learn to read. They read or write the same story over and over again, as though to practice the act of reading. While the repetitive movement or figure seems the same, in fact, there is something new or different with each repetition. In the therapy room, repetition provides a structure while the child probes, explores, and rehearses a new way of being around a difficult situation. With time, the energy around a difficult situation shifts.

Case study: the lizard

Rachael, a nine-year-old girl, exemplified this repetitive use of symbol through a series of monster drawings completed over a period of a year.

In our first session, I asked Rachael to draw a picture of herself as a monster. She looked up at me wide-eyed and then began to put pastel to paper. She drew a very cute, smiling, yellow lizard with green scales. It stood alone on the empty page. There was no background, but coming from the lizard's mouth was a small bubble. The iguana said "eerrr." The iguana felt very delicate and the expression looked and sounded very repressed to me. I even asked Rachael to repeat the sound and again, she looked up at me with a voice softer than her speaking voice, and again said "eerrr."

Several months later, Rachael was asked to complete the "monster drawing" again. The exact same iguana shape appeared in her picture. This time the lizard was blue with green spikes. It was surrounded by outlines of billowy gray clouds and a large sun. No words came out of her mouth, but when asked what the lizard was saying, Rachael said "Where's my child?"

The same lizard appeared in the third drawing, in a different color scheme. The sun was now on the other side of the picture and the entire picture had color. The lizard stood on the ground, and had legs that seemed to be moving. The lizard now said "yaka do, yaka do; yaka yaka yaka do!" Rachael said these words with complete enthusiasm. She said them with power and strength.

Commentary

The lizard form had remained constant, while the color, background, and voice changed over time. Again, feeling the energy of the child was important. Each drawing was energetically more powerful than the one before. I felt the shift in Rachael, not so much through the form of the lizard, but by what was going on in her environment and by the power in which she gave voice to her feelings. I was careful not to interpret, but rather to recognize and appreciate the changing tone of the monster drawing.

Movements of transformation

I have noticed many structural movements as children work with expressive arts and sandplay. Markell speaks about two of these transformational movements in her book, *Sand, Water, Silence* (2002). The first relates to the client's use of the center of the sand scene. She refers to this as a movement from concrete space to sacred space.

The center of the sandtray, according to Markell, is often experienced as a sanctuary. She believes that the "sacred center" is the essence of temenos. This is where "the intensity of these archetypal powers can be experienced in safety" (p.59). She says that the child often places an important symbol at the center of a sand scene, such as a sacred mountain, a pyramid, a temple, volcano, a tree, and something similar. In some cases, by contrast, this central location has been noticeably empty, as in the following example.

Case study: getting centered

Ronnie was a shy seven-year-old who lacked self-confidence. She enjoyed working with the sand tray and expressive arts material. After a few sessions, she began constructing a sand scene that repeated itself over the next few sessions. Miniatures were placed on mounds around the edge of the scene. A fire-pit was placed on one mound in the corner of the sand tray. When this scene was first created, small cats were placed on each mound. Some of the mounds had bridges connecting them. A trio of small cats was placed next to one mound. The center of the tray was noticeably empty. This basic structure was repeated over a three-month period of time. Each time it was repeated, the mounds with the cats on them would remain constant, but the trio of cats would get closer and closer to the center. One day the small cats were replaced by big, wild cats and the trio was placed in the center of the tray. Over time, the sand tray miniatures seemed to move closer to the fire-pit and the cats became larger and more animated.

Commentary

My intent here is not to interpret the sand scenes but to point out examples of sandplay where the center place has proved to be important to the process. Amy's center mound that appeared week after week was central to her healing process. Sue felt invited into sandplay by an energetic object that was present in the center of the tray, while Ronnie began to find her energetic self as she moved deeper and deeper into the center of the sandplay. As I work with young clients, I merely notice this movement and feel the energy that is present within the scenes. In each of these cases, activity or lack of activity at the center of the sand scene gives me insight into the inner world of the child and the healing process that is taking place.

Space–time dimensions of movements

Both sandplay therapists and expressive arts therapists understand the significance of moving through time and space in the healing process. Markell (2002) describes this as a "movement of transformation" and refers to *space–time dimensions of movements*. She explains that embodied involvement in the sand tray, combined with emotional participation, can bring about conditions conducive for healing. Experiencing this enables the client to begin to move from the concrete, literal expression to a more meaningful, symbolic understanding of life and personal narrative, whether or not this is spoken or just reflected in daily living (Markell 2002). When this movement occurs, the child becomes more conscious of their healing process.

Birth of the Courageous One

Matt began therapy at ten years old, owing to persistent bullying in school. He felt traumatized by this and "couldn't take it anymore." He often asked his teachers and parents for help when this happened. They supported him, which was helpful, but it also stifled his ability to stand up for himself. At the same time his mother was considering marrying her new boyfriend. Part of my work with Matt was to help him to develop his inner resources and courage to enable him to cope more easily with his life circumstances.

Matt's early scenes were all battles. They were dramatic and filled the entire tray. Initially, they were random, chaotic battles, but they became more and more focussed as his therapy progressed. One day, Matt took his finger and divided the tray into four quadrants. In each quadrant there was a very specific battle that he described in a story at the end. There was a sense that he was beginning to move from a general state of chaotic aggression toward a place where he was able to explore and transform specific struggles in his life.

A figure of a king that he named "The Courageous One" emerged one month after he had set up the battles in the four quadrants. This time he used five figures that were preparing to battle a snake, an octopus, and a giant spider. Although I typically do not engage in direct discussion during sandplay, when I noticed this unusual constellation of figures, I decided to seize the opportunity to discuss openly and to make conscious the qualities that Matt assigned to the five figures. He explained that a *black* figure was "the fighter" inside of him, a figure of a *swan* expressed the "gentle side of his nature," a *tiger* represented his "strength," a *goddess* was the "peacemaker," and a *red knight* was the part of him that was "courageous." This same knight was a constant figure in previous battle scenes when Matt had been dealing with difficult material.

With this in mind, Matt separated out the red knight from the rest of the scene, placed him on a platform, and spoke about him in more depth. We discussed the qualities that this figure possessed and what made him courageous. I asked Matt to describe times in his life when he had behaved in similar ways. He did. We explored these times more fully. He then began to playact the red knight, and ultimately dubbed the miniature with a name that reflected these qualities "The Courageous One."

At that moment, Matt gave birth to the Courageous One in a *conscious* way. My hope was that he would begin to identify with that part he had projected onto others and move the energy into his life situations. Soon after that, he accepted his mother's plans to remarry, and was better at coping with and thwarting the bullying behavior. He was also better able to deal with changes in his life circumstances. He had begun to develop inner resources.

Summary

This chapter has explored the importance of the arts and sandplay as powerful vehicles of healing and transformation. By creating a safe space for children to work symbolically, the therapist can observe and gently facilitate non-verbal and symbolic play. Transformation happens over time, as was shown in the examples, and the observant therapist quietly notices changes in the play without interpreting individual creative explorations or sand scenes. The transformative movements reveal the healing that is taking place over the course of many therapy sessions. An important role of the therapist is to watch and hold that sacred space so that healing can happen.

References

Clements, J. (2003) 'Organic inquiry: Research in partnership with Spirit.' Unpublished manuscript.

Kalff, D. (1991) 'Introduction to sandplay therapy.' *Journal of Sandplay Therapy 1*, 1, 7–15.

Knill, P.J. (1999) 'Soul nourishment, or the intermodal language of imagination.' In S.K. Levine and Ellen G. Levine (eds) *Foundations of Expressive Arts Therapy: Theoretical and Clinical Perspectives.* London: Jessica Kingsley Publishers.

Levine, E. (1999) 'On the playground: child psychotherapy and expressive arts therapy.' In S.K. Levine and Ellen G. Levine (eds) *Foundations of Expressive Arts Therapy: Theoretical and Clinical Perspectives.* London: Jessica Kingsley Publishers.

Mandelbaum, D. (2006) 'The therapeutic container in sandplay therapy: an exploration of psychospiritual space.' Unpublished doctoral dissertation, Institute of Transpersonal Psychology, Palo Alto, CA.

Markell, J. (2002) *Sand, Water, Silence: The Embodiment of Spirit: Explorations in Matter and Psyche.* London: Jessica Kingsley Publishers.

Metzner, R. (1986) *The Unfolding Self: Varieties of Transformative Experience.* Novato, CA: Origin Press.

McCarthy, D. (2007) *If You Turned into a Monster.* London: Jessica Kingsley Publishers.

McNiff, S. (1992) *Art as Medicine: Creating a Therapy of the Imagination.* Boston, MA: Shambhala Publications.

Rogers, C. (1990) *A Way of Being.* New York, NY: Houghton, Mifflin.

Rogers, N. (1997) *The Creative Connection: Expressive Arts as Healing.* Palo Alto, CA: Science and Behavior Books, Inc.

Rogers, N. (1999) '*The creative connection: a holistic expressive arts process.*' In S.K. Levine and Ellen G. Levine (eds) *Foundations of Expressive Arts Therapy: Theoretical and Clinical Perspectives.* London: Jessica Kingsley Publishers.

Rowe, N.M. (2005) 'Birth of the Courageous One: A case study that combines psychosynthesis and sandplay therapy.' *East Coast Sandplay Journal.*

Ryce-Menuhin (1992) *Jungian Sandplay: The Wonderful Therapy.* London: Routledge.

Signell, K. (1996) 'Silence and sandplay.' *Journal of Sandplay Therapy 5,* 2, 68–87.

Singer, J. (1994) *Boundaries of the Soul: The Practice of Jung's Psychology.* New York, NY: Anchor Books.

Taylor, J (2007) 'Personal communication.' Workshop.

Chapter 9

Getting to the Core
Moving through the Language Barrier

Noelle Ghnassia Damon

Robert's parents decided that the nightmares needed to stop. At the age of four Robert was having difficulty every night with nightmares that would awaken and frighten him and render his parents powerless to help. No amount of companionship, comfort, or light would help him get through the night. During the day he appeared agitated, restless, distracted in school, and extremely fearful of bedtime. Medicines were administered, despite his young age. Though his behavior in school became more manageable and compliant, behind the well-behaved façade resided fear, a fear that visited him every night.

This is the story of a child, one of many, who had been plagued by fear at an early age. With the help of non-verbal therapies that included EMDR (Eye Movement Desensitization and Reprocessing) he was able to release the emotional intensity of his early childhood experiences to return to his vital energy core.

By the time Robert was brought in to see me he had already been in treatment for nearly a year. His nightmares began when he was around two, and his father and stepmother were led by his pediatrician to believe that he would outgrow them. In fact, he did not outgrow them and they became more disturbing and carried over into his daily functioning. Over the next year he was seen by a pediatric neurologist, a psychiatrist, and a psychotherapist. He was diagnosed with ADHD (attention deficit and hyperactivity disorder) and placed on medication. When the medication did not effectively eliminate the problem, he was scheduled to be seen regularly by a child psychotherapist. With his therapist he had engaged in play activities consisting primarily of board games. Parent interviews had been conducted and histories were taken. It was disclosed that Robert had been exposed to extremely violent behavior during his parents' divorce, and later while alone in his mother's care. He had been separated from his mother when his father received full custody and he saw her only during supervised visits. It was at that time that his anxiety became more pronounced and his sleep became severely disturbed. He carried with him both the loss of his mother and his fear of her. It was this combination of grief and fear that made Robert unable to adapt to his safer existence at home and continued to make him feel that he was in imminent danger.

Words are laden with architecture and meaning which construct perceptions of reality but often cannot express the subtleties of human experience. We as therapists can liberate our clients from the constructs of language by connecting them to the essence of the subtle energy of their souls. Non-verbal therapy allows contact with the collective unconscious and brings knowledge to the individual with energy rather than mere structure or language. Ultimately, we learn with the heart the lessons gleaned from experience.

For the purposes of this chapter, because many other non-verbal therapies are discussed within this book, I will look at Robert's case primarily from the perspective of EMDR and trauma theory. I juxtapose the concepts of EMDR and the soul to explain the mechanics that are involved in reducing disturbance levels and balancing the energy that is essential for healing. It is the premise of this unified field theory approach that the brain can instinctively process new information and heal itself when the optimal conditions are provided.

An event that is perceived as traumatic is frequently stored, almost in its original form, in a neural network that is locked deep within the nervous system, away from the brain's cognitive processes. An event that is experienced as serious loss that is overwhelming, sudden, unexpected, violent, forceful, or is a challenge to one's safety, may be considered as traumatic. The images, thoughts, sounds, smells, emotions, physical sensations, and beliefs about oneself get stored all together in the emotional mute brain which is separate from the conscious, logical, verbal brain. It is for that reason that traumatic memories lack a verbal narrative and context and are encoded in the form of vivid sensations and images (Brett and Ostroff 1985).

EMDR is a trauma-based therapy that was developed by Dr Francine Shapiro in 1987 when she began her research into the field of adaptive information processing. Working with Vietnam veterans, she concluded by

1989 that bilateral brain stimulation by means of back-and-forth eye movements could help to desensitize disturbing memories and effectively reprocess them in a positively adapted form. The premise of EMDR (Shapiro 2001) is that processed memories are the basis of health, and stored but unprocessed memories are the basis of pathology. Dysfunctional and pathological traits, behaviors, beliefs, actions, and body sensations are believed to be results of these unprocessed memories. Disturbance will continue until they are accessed and processed. EMDR uses trauma-based assessment to look at how the person was traumatized and then works to eliminate those sources of trauma by desensitizing and reprocessing those memories.

The brain comprises roughly 100 billion neurons, each with 100 to 10,000 synapses. Memory depends on the synaptic connections created between brain cells. When cells are activated simultaneously by trauma they become connected by association and therefore create a semi-permanent neural network which becomes an unprocessed, dysfunctional, and volatile packet of information that can be reactivated at the slightest reminder of the event. A smell, image, or touch can trigger other neurons which are connected to the physical sensations of the memory of the original event, and in a flash the smell of smoke, for example, could evoke fear. The instantaneous reaction is completed by hormonal cascading of the limbic system, which causes the person to experience a level of disturbance which may be equivalent to that felt at the time of the original event. This is the nature of flashbacks, memories that continue to be experienced as if they are in the present, otherwise known as "frozen procedural memories."

Bessel van der Kolk (1994) explains that traumatic memories are not narrative in nature. Initially they are stored as somato-sensory fragments, as non-declarative or implicit memory, within the emotional brain. It is the goal of most therapies to help restore emotional health by moving stored, disturbing memories from *implicit (unconscious, procedural)* memory to *explicit (conscious, declarative)* memory. This allows the logical, rational brain (the language center) to create a healing narrative, an adaptive processing, of the stored information, and to reconnect oneself back to one's core energy, one's soul. Each psychotherapy modality has its own hypotheses, premises, and protocols to accomplish that goal. Whichever way it is done, it has been found that the most effective treatments are those that bypass language and access the frozen procedural memories (lodged in the emotional brain) through other pathways.

My work moves beyond the language barrier to speak with the soul. Gary Zukav, in *The Seat of the Soul* (1989), defines the soul as the energy core.

The soul is the core aspect of each person's human presence. It is knowable through a felt-sense and is a non-intellectual experience of body–mind feelings. It is when one loses connection to one's center that one loses connection to one's own ways of knowing, and to one's place where one can feel renewed, resourceful, and content (Gilligan 1977). It must be through one's felt-sense, through one's intuitive self, that access to the soul is gained. The body has its own natural wisdom and intuitive integrative capacity. It is to that wisdom and that center that I bring my client back into connection. Authentic empowerment is ultimately the alignment of the personality with the soul (Zukav 1989), the communication between the extrinsic self and the intrinsic self, that which is observable and conscious and that which resides deep within us. It is this alignment that brings health, resilience, and openness to new experiences to the individual, adult, and child alike.

Children, having walked the earth for less time than adults, have less material obstructing their connections to their souls, their centers, which is why they come to this place of being so naturally. The personality hasn't yet created defenses and obstacles so impenetrable that access to the core is blocked. It is, however, incumbent upon the therapist to use methods which communicate with the core, and to be careful not to follow the client's words too literally, so that attention does not move further away from the core. It is for this reason that I bring attention back to the felt-sense, back to the place in the somatic self that has a sense of knowing and responding effectively to the world.

With EMDR, bilateral brain stimulation (eye movement, or alternating physical tapping or audible sounds) creates the optimal condition (thought to be similar to the REM (rapid eye movement) stage of sleep), for the brain to accelerate processing and create a qualitative shift in the brain. Bringing awareness to the body, attention to the felt-sense, as well as images and beliefs, EMDR shifts the frozen procedural memory from the mute part of the brain to the language-based, cognitive side of the brain.

PET (position emission tomography) scans of the brains of traumatized individuals pre- and post-treatment with EMDR have shown a change in the area of brain activity when exposed to reminders of trauma. The pre-treatment images showed activity in the area of the posterior right brain (the amygdala and the visual cortex) and the post-treatment scans showed activity in the anterior left area of the brain (the prefrontal cortex). This in fact demonstrates that the traumatic memory is originally lodged in the area of the brain most closely related to the neurobiological functioning of the body and most distant from the verbal, intellectual brain functioning. It is also observed that in the pre-test images the area of the brain which controls speech (Broca's area, the left prefrontal cortex) looks the way that it does when it is anesthetized, while the visual cortex is activated in the same manner as when it is when presented with a photograph. Traumatic memories, then, have very little, if any, verbal representation and are located in bodily states and unconscious patterns of behavior. EMDR creates a shift in the memory storage and enables a person to live in the present, open to new experiences, and able to learn from old experiences that they can leave behind (van der Kolk 1998).

Robert Scaer M.D., a neurologist who has developed a theory based on the neurophysiology of traumatic stress, posits that many chronic diseases with unknown causes are related to unresolved traumatic experiences. He has concluded from his years of research that if memories are not adequately discharged they will continue to be activated, to emerge, and to disturb when triggered by environmental cues, and will eventually create a process he calls "kindling." Kindling is the establishment of an internal, self-perpetuating neural circuit that contributes to ongoing, often permanent symptoms, both physiological and psychological (Scaer 2006). The effects of trauma on brain development show interference in the limbic system (causing increased irritability, greater aggression, and self-destructive tendencies), arrested development of the left hemisphere (responsible for symptoms of depression, memory impairment, learning disabilities), and compromised corpus callosum (difficulty integrating right and left hemispheres, often resulting in dramatic shifts in personality and mood). With early childhood trauma, the interference from the kindling process (a perpetually aroused amygdala and a shrunken hippocampus) causes disruption in the normal brain processes required for healthy development and sets the stage for learning disabilities, emotional dysregulation, and a compromised immune system.

Returning to the case of Robert, we can see that the agitation, irritability, and poor concentration in school that he exhibited were a result of PTSD (post-traumatic stress disorder), and not ADHD. The diagnoses that he had been given were related to his presenting symptoms and did not take into account the effects of his earlier experiences on the overall functioning of his brain. Diagnoses often given to children frequently underestimate, or completely ignore, the damage that early childhood trauma causes in the developing brain. The treatments attempt to eliminate symptom sets, yet neglect to treat their underlying causes. Treatments which "talk" to the symptoms are largely responsible for the proliferation of these diagnoses: behavior management, cognitive behavioral therapy, and psychopharmacological treatment. These therapies may be effective, but are often not enough, or require lengthy treatment, with mixed results. Therapies that propose to "speak" to the unspeakable, to address the hidden causes, to discharge the intensity of the implicit memories, and to reconnect the person with their soul, understand that the disturbance resides deep within the fabric of the body and the mind, and set out to eliminate the root causes.

Non-verbal therapy is not conducted in silence but it is understood that words alone will not provide the basis for change. Change can only be effected if the child is able to reach deeply into their emotional, imaginal world. Adults, with years of language behind them, have ways of understanding and expressing emotion that may offer the opportunity to shift cognitive and behavioral patterns. Yet even with sophisticated language it can take years of talk-therapy to bring about the positive adaptive behavior that is sought. This is in part why non-verbal therapies such as EMDR, somatic experiencing, mindfulness training, guided meditation, sandplay therapy, and creative expressive therapy (among others) are also readily used with adults.

When I am present for a client I use my energy to attune to their process. This involves listening with my heart and mind—with my emotional intelligence and my conscious intelligence. Through the use of playful connection, I guide the client toward their lost center. I bear witness to their present experience and offer them tools that move beyond the confines of language. Body-centered therapy, sandplay, creative and expressive arts therapies provide them with symbols with which they can bring their inside out. In so doing, they bear witness to themselves and come closer to their own internal natural order, one with coherence and harmonic resonance—self-made rather than externally imposed. In this work there are no judgments, interpretations, nor assigning of blame; there is only the respectful observance of a person's process and the acceptance of unfolding knowledge.

Case study: Robert

Robert started working with me after his previous therapist had left the area. With time he adjusted to me and to my office, and our therapeutic rapport became stronger with every session. He would walk cautiously down the hall to my office, sometimes in his pajamas, depending on the hour of the session. He cracked a smile for me each time, but quickly reverted to his serious demeanor, exhibiting little facial expression except a small furrow of his brow. He was a mature child, living among adults, with few children his age with whom to play. Though he was in school, his working parents didn't have time to set up play dates for him. His language skills were very well developed for his age and his father was pleased with what a little man he was. He navigated his world, however, with trepidation and caution, in a way that would suggest that he was perpetually weighing the consequences of his actions and the safety of his environment. It was his game playing which demonstrated his social skills the best. He loved to play board games, as he had with his previous therapist. He demonstrated a good sense of humor as he got closer to winning. He stoically accepted his losses, but he was sullen when he lost and would worry about his failure and insist on another chance to redeem himself. Winning, for him, was an indication of mastery, and his worry would then fade. His victories, however, were only temporary; he would leave feeling triumphant, but return home only to be faced by his fear-filled nights.

Over time, I moved our activities during sessions away from his old familiar ways of board game playing to more body-oriented, somatically-centered activities in order to move his experience of himself from his head back into his body. We initially did this by playing hide-and-seek—his choice of activity. It is always interesting to see what forms of play the child will choose, as these are most often indicative of the developmental stage where growth was arrested or hindered. In my little office Robert would find places behind chairs, under desks, and in closets to hide and surprise. He took great pleasure in this activity and would never tire of it.

I understood this as his need to recreate the play of his infancy within a safer and more predictable environment than he had had at that age. He was reorienting himself and rebuilding the foundation of his energetic core. This work is essential in EMDR; one must have a solid connection to one's strengths and resources before desensitization and reprocessing of old memories is done. This is similar to other therapeutic methods that do not remove defenses until new insights or skills are in place. With adults this is achieved by exploring their accomplishments, their successes, their areas of mastery, and helping them find positive experiences in their everyday lives. With children, and often with adults as well, it frequently requires revisiting earlier developmental stages through play, imagination, guided imagery, and artistic expression, to build a new foundation of experience that is positive and upon which future experiences can be laid. In this way the memory banks begin to fill with bundles of positive associations which will later be useful in reprocessing old memories. So, in this way, Robert's play became more full-bodied, less cerebral, and his four-year-old self was feeling more free to express himself, yet he always reined himself back in when it was time to leave the session.

When we saw each other regularly, Robert looked refreshed. When he missed a session or two he would arrive looking drawn, tired, and weary from worry. He carried the burden of a child who had seen too much and his days were filled with the demands of coping. He was continuing to do well in school and he was social and well-behaved. His parents and doctors kept him on medication. His defense was to remain serious, guarded, and always prepared for the worst. His medication eased some of his hypervigilance but his serious, alert nature remained. With me he allowed himself to be more playful, yet outside he was greatly defended. Though it was taking time, he was developing internal strength with every session by exploring and expressing the uninhibited, intuitive self at his core. He would jump up and down for no reason, and then jump for joy, throw a ball, and then drop to the ground and wiggle around. He giggled and made baby noises, he babbled and cooed. His instinctive nature was building upon itself from the inside out in a slow, progressive fashion. His energetic core was emerging. As Alexander Lowen proposes, children manifest in their games and play the creative impulse at work in the human personality: "The ease with which a child can pretend or make believe indicates that his world is largely an inner one containing a rich store of feelings upon which he can draw" (1970, p. 15). When Robert began therapy he was unable to access his imagination or his joy due to early childhood trauma. His feelings were inaccessible because they were mainly composed of the feeling of fear, to which he remained as closed as possible. With time and attunement to his needs and his readiness, he began to open himself to his inner world and his potential to experience a full array of emotions and feelings.

I met frequently with his parents as well during that time, in order to address their own fears, grief, and anger. They worried that he would never get better and that he would always exhibit anxiety. They harbored resentment toward his mother and unknowingly fueled his internal conflicts. I addressed their feelings and pointed out the large part their own feelings and behaviors played in his emotional development. Rather than focusing on neglect and abuse on the part of Robert's mother, we discussed the consistent support, redirection, and playfulness they could now offer him. Introducing levity in their home was essential—and difficult, because the tensions between his biological parents reverberated after each supervised visit, after each phone call, after each nightmare. Robert's father and stepmother (who demonstrated great love and affection for him) were continually worried for him and he followed suit. They all resided in worry, and so were encouraged to exercise choices that would shift their focus to playful attention. In order to do this the parents needed to have trust: trust in me, in Robert, and, most important, in themselves. Slowly, they began to reframe some of their experiences and they purposefully chose nurturance and playfulness over morbid curiosity and anger when speaking with Robert about his experiences with his mother, or his nightmares.

Robert responded well to bio-energetic movement and to symbolic play. He explored the sand table and replicated his interactive play in the sand. His game of hide-and-seek continued with burying and uncovering little artifacts, marbles, coins, and game pieces. He would bury them and ask me to find them. While I looked, he would crawl around the room and pretend he was an animal and ask me to guess which one he was. In this way he was saying "Find me!" and "Help me find myself!" He was simultaneously expanding his energetic expression, his imagination, and his connection to his core self.

Eventually, as time went on, he would come skipping down the hall when it was session time, wearing a big grin on his face. He would jump up for a hug and begin talking about what he wanted to do during our time together. His defenses were softening and his creative, authentic expression was emerging. However, his nightmares were persisting and immoveable. His parents continued to report on his poor nights' sleep and his fearful fits of restlessness. He himself never spoke about them and one would guess from the quality of his interaction with me that they didn't exist. At my suggestion the parents stopped trying to make him talk about his nightmares and simply let him "shake them off" when he awakened. "Shaking off" is tantamount to discharging energy and is imperative for the proper release of tension and residual trauma, as described by Peter Levine (2005) in his Somatic Experiencing Therapy. Now mornings brought a wiggly shake-off dance in Robert's kitchen and songs to chase away the feelings of the night. Robert no longer had the negative carry-over into his day, but his parents still agreed the nightmares needed to stop.

After months of individual sessions with Robert, and parent counseling sessions with his parents, Robert had been progressing well. He had initially learned to hide behind his words and his stiffened, joyless body, but he was now engaging well, had become more expressive with his body, and had begun to release some of the rigidity connected with his verbal presentation to the world. He was still logical and continued to create well thought out arguments when discussing his needs with his parents. The only exception was bedtime and nighttime. It was then that his unconscious world revealed itself and his logical mind could not control it. This conflict caused even more distress. Now was a good time to do the desensitization and reprocessing part of our EMDR work.

I had introduced EMDR to Robert's parents early in his treatment and explored it further as the time became appropriate to do the bilateral brain stimulation (BLS), which in Robert's case took the form of alternate tapping on his knees. EMDR combines a somatic therapeutic approach with eye movement or rhythmical stimulation to integrate both hemispheres of the brain. For Robert it was like another game which would involve some tapping and some drawing. EMDR is an eight-phase psychotherapy treatment, and we had already completed the first two phases. The first included the history taking, trauma assessment, rapport building, and strengths assessment and building. The second was the preparation phase, in which there was the creation of a positive memory network, coping skills, self-soothing, de-escalation tactics, body awareness, imagery work, and establishment of a safe place. The safe place in many cases is an imaginary place. For Robert it was my office, as it was easy for him to picture.

During the next few phases of our work, having already identified the target (the nightmare) that we would desensitize, I would help him come up with a subjective measure of disturbance. We would identify what he believed about himself, what he would like to believe about himself instead, and then desensitize with BLS. We would reprocess the memory with his desired belief about himself and then scan his body for any residual areas of disturbance. It is important to note that the therapist is setting the stage for the mind and body to do their own work, and nothing is imposed on the client. It is all coming from the instinctive abilities of the being to heal itself. The therapist sets the scene and encourages the client to allow their mind and body to go where they need to go, allowing the right brain to communicate with the left brain, and the soul and personality to come into dialogue. The observing mind (the soul) becomes aligned with the personality, the target memory gets desensitized and then reprocessed in a fully adaptive manner, and in this way healing takes place.

I had asked that Robert's parents attend the session that evening to witness and assist. I had told Robert that our next session was going to be different and that his parents would be coming in with him so that we could talk to the nightmares. He didn't want to talk about them or to them, but agreed that we could.

When he arrived, Robert was in his pajamas, bathed, fed, and ready for bed. His parents' schedule was such that he frequently came to see me after dinner and close to bedtime. That evening they sat in my office with an air of expectancy and some apprehension. His nightmares were going to be "spoken" to that night, and that meant they too would be present. Robert had never admitted them into our sessions before. I told him how brave I believed he was being that night, and assured him that we were all there with him and would keep him safe. With his parents seated on either side of him, he and I explored ways of describing and measuring levels of disturbance. Using the floor and the ceiling to measure how much it disturbed him, he described his nightmare as bothering him as much as was feasibly possible; his arms stretched up toward the ceiling, and furrowing his brow, he pointed and said, "That much!" I asked him how he felt and he said, "Scared" and said that he thought "the bad guys can get me in my room at night." When I asked him what he would like to think he said, "That I'm okay. Daddy and Mommy are here and no one can get me!" Giving him a different way to measure the validity of his belief, using his hands in front of him, closer or farther apart, I asked him to tell me how true that felt when he thought about being in his room at night. With his hands he showed that it was a little true, about as big as a lunchbox. Next I asked if he could draw a picture of the most upsetting part of his nightmares. He proceeded to draw a simple picture with a line on the bottom of the page for his bed and then a circle above it with a scowling face inside. He said it was the face he saw on his wall every night that made him scared, and he didn't want to talk about it any more because he was getting scared and this wasn't fun! I assured him that we wouldn't talk about the nightmare anymore, but I needed to ask him a question about his body. He agreed to continue, and I asked him where he felt it in his body when he thought about his nightmare. He took a moment and then responded that it was in his head and stomach.

Robert, seated on a small chair in front of his parents, felt their presence as the weight of their hands rested on his shoulders. He looked trusting yet bewildered as I explained that we were going to face his night-mares together and try to make them stop bothering him. I asked him to hold the picture of the nightmare in his head, along with his thought that the bad guys could get him, and told him he could let his pictures and thoughts go wherever they wanted as soon as I started tapping his knees. He was very serious and said, "Okay," with a look of concentration on his face. He reached up and held his parents' arms as they continued to touch his shoulders, and he watched as I tapped on his knees. I asked after about 30 seconds what he noticed was happening to the pictures, the feelings, and the thoughts, and he said, "They're going away." We continued for a few more sets. Each time he said, "They're going away," and finally he said, "They're gone! I can't see them." I asked if he would like to draw a picture of what he did see, and he drew the same thing, but this time the circle had nothing inside. "They're really gone!" he exclaimed. He knew what he had seen in his head, but as soon as he saw it on paper it became real to him. I asked how much it was now bothering him, again indicating the ceiling and the floor to measure the disturbance level. Robert motioned proudly with his hands as he put them on the floor and then turned them over, shrugged his shoulders and said, "It doesn't bother me now." I then asked him how he felt in his body, and he said, "Okay." How were his stomach and his head feeling? He said, "Good." I then asked him to think about his thought, "*I'm okay. Daddy and Mommy are here and no one can get me*," and asked how true that was. He threw his arms out as wide as possible and with a big grin on his face said, "This much!" then turned around and hugged his stepmother.

The desensitization was complete, and as seen here, it can be very rapid in children because they have such short memory channels. All that was needed for completion was the reprocessing of the nightmare (the target) with his positive belief. We would consolidate the desensitized memory with his newly formed, firm belief about himself, "*I'm okay. Daddy and Mommy are here and no one can get me*." In this way we altered the disabling core belief at the center of his memory. Resuming our positions, I asked him to hold the picture of the nightmare in his head, along with the good feeling in his body and the statement, "*I'm okay. Daddy and Mommy are here and no one can get me*," and then I did another slower set of tapping (the set rates vary, depending on what part of the process you are completing). With this completed, I asked Robert one more time what he was noticing, and he said he was happy and the nightmare picture went away. The test, of course, was how he would feel when he went to bed that night and subsequent nights. I would follow up the next day and again the following week.

I received a call from his parents the next day stating he had slept soundly through the night and they were delighted. He awakened the next morning and did his "shake-off" dance as usual, but this time because he was happy. The following week he woke in the night a number of times but was able to fall back to sleep with the comfort and companionship of his parents. No faces remained on the walls and no unmanageable fears haunted him at night. His parents were able to comfort him when he did awaken, and they all reveled in that.

Supervised visits with Robert's mother continued, and phone calls triggered more tensions in the home, but when problems arose they never escalated to the level that they had before. His early childhood trauma had been resolved, his core beliefs transformed, his foundation consolidated, and his family empowered to meet his needs and growing self.

The last time I saw Robert he was in clothes that he had gotten dirty from a good day of work and play. At the end of our last session, as I crouched down to his level, he gave me a long hug, keeping his feet firmly on the ground. As he walked away holding his parents' hands, he raised his head, looked from one parent to the other, and smiled. Robert had authentically moved beyond the confines of language and found his centered self.

References

Brett, E.A. and Ostroff, R. (1985) "Imagery in post-traumatic stress disorder: an overview." *American Journal of Psychiatry 142*, 417–424.

Discover Magazine (2007) 'Ten unsolved mysteries of the brain.' August, p.56.

Gilligan, S. (1977) *The Courage to Love. Principles and Practices of Self-Relations Psychotherapy.* New York, NY and London: W.W. Norton and Company.

Levine, P.A. (2005) *Healing Trauma: A Pioneering Program for Restoring the Wisdom of the Body.* Boulder, CO: Sounds True.

Lowen, A. (1970) *Pleasure.* New York, NY: Lancer Books.

Scaer, R. (2006) 'The neurophysiology of healing.' Conference conducted by the EMDR International Association, Philadelphia, PA.

Shapiro, F. (2001) *Eye Movement Desensitization and Reprocessing: Basic Principles, Protocols and Procedures* (2nd ed.). New York, NY: Guilford Press.

van der Kolk, B.A. (1994) 'The body keeps the score: memory and the emerging psychobiology of PTSD.' *Harvard Review of Psychiatry 1*, 253–265.

van der Kolk, B.A. (1998) 'Understanding the psychobiology of trauma.' Conference conducted by the EMDR International Association, Baltimore, MD.

Zukav, G. (1989) *The Seat of The Soul.* New York, NY: Fireside (First Fireside edition, 1990).

Further reading

Pearsall, P. (1998) *The Heart's Code. The New Findings about Cellular Memories and their Role in the Mind/Body/Spirit Connection.* New York, NY: Broadway Books.

Servan-Schreiber, D. (2004) *The Instinct to Heal. Curing Depression, Anxiety, and Stress Without Drugs and without Talk Therapy.* USA, Rodale, originally published in French by Editions Robert Laffont, Paris, 2003.

Shapiro, F. and Forrest, M.S. (1997) *EMDR: The Breakthrough Therapy for Overcoming Anxiety, Stress and Trauma.* New York: Basic Books.

van der Kolk, B.A. (1996) *Traumatic Stress. The Effects of Overwhelming Experience on Mind, Body, and Society.* New York, NY: Guilford Press.

Chapter 10

Quicksand!
Provocation to Change

Dennis McCarthy

Much in life provokes us to change and grow; physical and/or psychological symptoms, difficult life situations we find ourselves in, troubled relationships, or impasses on the normal road to development. In other words, all the potentially "bad" things that happen to us offer us the chance to grow if we are able to use them as such. Whatever unsettles us opens the door for a new way.

Dreams offer us a similar and often nightly experience of this, without the overt negative associations that the above life-altering situations bring. And it is often dreams we reject as not us or anti-us or insignificant that have this paradoxical, unsettling yet life-affirming power. These images loosen the hold our defense system has on us, at least potentially and momentarily, as well as the blocks inhibiting us from change.

The act of provocation elicited by the dreams we have, or play configurations we create, often needs the presence of "the other" to help us enter into these images or access the energy they contain. The image itself is provocative and the alignment of a therapist with the provocative image further intensifies this.

Children rarely feel threatened by the images they create in the way that adults often do, having less of a fixed sense of who they are, yet children also benefit from our presence, our vision, our containment of the image's energy, and our willingness to consider how the image might be utilized. This last part is central. We must help the child consider how the image might be used. This needn't happen with words, or at least not with a direct interpretation. We might offer a play form that will facilitate this, if the child does not. We might encourage a furthering of the story, either by suggesting it come to life or evolve into the next chapter. It is not really a passive role that we play in my experience, either with adults or with children.

Almost any image is potentially unsettling, depending on the context and our associations with it. Images that describe an energetic experience, or contain movement in them in an obvious way, or describe a form-altering process, are particularly provocative. Tidal wave dreams are one example of this and are quite frequent in adults. Usually they predate the beginning of therapy and often they have been happening for many years. They seem purely negative at first glance, threatening to annihilate life as we know it, and yet because of the immense power they describe and also their sense of inescapableness, they provoke change. We must contend with them. They must be heeded in some way, and they often come again and again until we do at least consider them.

One woman had tidal waves dreams from puberty onwards. They intensified at times in her life when she was stuck. Her tidal waves always chased her across the land, leaving others alone and focussing on her. She came to call them "my waves" and to be thrilled as well as terrified at their enormity and their relevance to her. As she deepened through her therapy process, they changed in tenor with her often swimming in them or riding on them rather than running from them. Only when she terminated therapy prematurely did the negative wave image return briefly. After resuming treatment, the waves once again became negotiable. For her the waves represented her thwarted sexuality and the need to assert herself. As she wrestled with these issues the energy that the wave contained became hers.

In sandplay, volcanoes are one frequently used image that invites and/or provokes change in a similar way to the tidal wave. The difference is that children build the volcano themselves as well as cause the eruption that ensues. Thus they connect to its power more easily, more willingly. The eruption may replicate many things; it can be the expression of rage and/or revenge, it can express the desire to shift form, or it may herald a new level of aggressivity being played with. In life, volcanic eruptions, although dreaded, do create new landmasses, often leaving very fertile soil in their wakes. There are many creation myths associated with them in lands where people live with the reality of these periodic eruptions.

Quicksand is one of the most peculiar, as well as one of the most often used, provocative images in sandplay. It is usually not a highlight but rather a momentary aside, a humorous/aggressive diversion, a chance for revenge or for the quick disposal of someone or many someones, a shift in consciousness, a shift from the solid to the liquid. It may lead to new and deeper levels of consciousness. It may provoke a sinking and yet also a rising of new energies. It is a paradox, and therein lies its power. And if we free-associate on the actual phenomena of quicksand, the psychological allusions are very rich. These associations are really the "meaning" of symbols. In the context of the data of a child's life story, of the process they have begun with us, these associations take on a charge, a meaning.

The following series of quicksand descriptions and definitions offer a wonderful parallel to the psychic associations we might attribute to the symbol.

> Quicksand is not quite the fearsome force of nature that you sometimes see on the big screen. In fact, quicksand is rarely deeper than a few feet. It can occur almost anywhere if the right conditions are present. Quicksand is basically just ordinary sand that has been so saturated with water that the friction between sand particles is reduced. The resulting sand is a mushy mixture of sand and water that can no longer support any weight.

> If you step into quicksand, it won't suck you down. However, your movements will cause you to dig yourself deeper into it. Quicksand is an interesting natural phenomenon—it is actually solid ground that has been liquified by an oversaturation of water. The "quick" refers to how easily the sand shifts when in this semiliquid state.

> Quicksand is not a unique type of soil; it is usually just sand or another type of grainy soil. Quicksand is nothing more than a soupy mixture of sand and water—in essence, the sand is floating on water. It can occur anywhere under the right conditions. (Denise Dumouchelle, United States Geological Survey (USGS), in Bonsor 2006)

Quicksand is created when water saturates an area of loose sand and the ordinary sand is agitated. When the water trapped in the batch of sand can't escape, it creates liquefied soil that can no longer support weight. There are two ways in which sand can become agitated enough to create quicksand:

Flowing underground water—the force of the upward water flow opposes the force of gravity, causing the granules of sand to be more buoyant.

Earthquakes—the force of the shaking ground can increase the pressure of shallow groundwater, which liquefies sand and silt deposits. The liquefied surface loses strength, causing buildings or other objects on that surface to sink or fall over. Vibration tends to enhance the quickness, so what is reasonably solid initially may become soft and then quick. (Larry Barron, New South Wales Geological Survey)

The vibration plus the water barrier reduces the friction between the sand particles and causes the sand to behave like a liquid. To understand quicksand, you have to understand the process of liquefaction. When soil liquefies, as with quicksand, it loses strength and behaves like a viscous liquid rather than a solid. (Utah Geological Survey, in Bonsor 2006)

The quicksand of dream, play configuration, and myth is just that—a myth. Its meaning is in its psychological relevance rather than its external reality, except that the actual phenomenon is strangely descriptive of the energetic shifts that provoke and foster change in us. Perhaps the fiction that quicksand has become is a result of the meanings we attribute to it. It resonates within us, conjuring up images of entrapment, suffocation, and futile struggle. And herein lies its regenerative power as an image. The state of absolute stuckness it puts us in forces change or death, at least in our fantasy. In actuality, to escape from quicksand, the trick is to relax. This is in and of itself an interesting paradox: relaxing into it frees us from it. Sinking via relaxation helps us to rise up out of it. The act of calling for help, if we are someone who needs to learn to do so, can also be what frees us.

Case study: David

Twelve-year-old David came for therapy due to poor school performance and an air of depression that had his mother very concerned. His father had died immediately after David's birth and he lived alone with his mother. In our first visit David described himself as afflicted with "the blahs." When I asked him if "the blahs" were coming from inside of him or outside, he thought for some time and then responded that it was both. The outside source was at least in part due to the constant bullying he was subjected to in school as well as his own thwarted aggression that prevented him from responding to this bullying, despite his mother's having given her blessing for any fights he needed to have to correct the situation. His inner-directed aggression was also contributing to the inner blahs, as well as the absence of father and maleness in his life.

David had a rather limp quality to his musculature. His facial expression was a bit sardonic. He was, however, very willing to make a scene in the sand, and his opening sand scene was also very blah, with some random figures set up without any story or "charge" to them. But something had been stirred up, for when he returned the next week he made the following scene:

> A graveyard is on one side of the box where the skeleton of a dead and buried knight lies in chains. On the other side of the box a living but captured knight is also in chains. Two other knights are approaching.

He had actually brought two small plastic chains with him from home to attach to the figures. He had clearly been planning a scene depicting enchainment. David whistled while he made the scene, but it was hair-raising in its depiction of the psychic state of his inner father–son relationship. Something had hooked him in our first visit, perhaps our chat about the blahs or my recognition of his potential to come back to life, and it allowed him to begin to imagine without realizing it what the problem was, or at least how he experienced it. The next week he made the following scene:

> Several battles are going on between groups of knights, knights and dragons, and knights and a god. In the center of the scene is a very large patch of quicksand, created by a god to trap people. Someone has fallen into it and many others have come to try to pull him out.

In this scene David's quicksand, attributed to a god (actually the god Shiva) functioned as a catalyst. It triggered action on the part of the helpers. It brought new energy to the surface, even as the figure depicted is sinking. This paradoxical energetic nature of the substance is part of its power. It represents both sinking and a rising in response to this. The battling groups of knights are a positive evolution of the dead and enchained knights of his previous scene.

David was really stuck in his life energetically and emotionally. But for me to push him to be more assertive was not what was needed, although of course my having that as an unspoken goal was important. David first needed to articulate his psychic reality via the dead and dying enchained knights and then the trapped figure. This was essential. He had to bring many things to life besides his aggression, such as his grief over the death of his father, and a longing to live more fully.

His next scene depicted a large volcano that erupted monsters rather than lava. Numerous figures were shown running from these volcanic monsters. The unleashed aggression in this was awesome. Would he be able to handle it? Would his mother? Subsequent sessions saw an evolution and refinement of this aggression via his scenes. He pushed against me, alternately rejecting me in one session and then bringing me strawberries a few times later. I further provoked him by insisting on bringing up his father periodically.

A summer camp experience in a very supportive wilderness camp for boys further solidified David's positive identification with the living masculine. He came back stirred up and ready for more. After several more visits he made the following scene:

> Hundreds of fighting figures fill the box. They run the gamut from cavemen with clubs, knights, Civil War figures, World War I and II army men, Indians, etc. There is layer upon layer of aggression. They are intertwined and overlapping in their battling of each other, and in the midst of these fighters are dragons, dinosaurs, and wild animals attacking them all. Astronauts land in their rocket ship and come out to explore and an alien spacecraft does as well. Above these all stands a devil on one side and an angel standing on a devil on the other side.

David was quite thrilled with his scene. He kept referring to it while he was making it as "chaos." He whistled and laughed while he made it. When he was done he called it "Pandora's box" and told me that this is what it looked and felt like inside of that mythic box. Then he quizzed me on my Greek myth knowledge by asking me if I knew what the last object was that was left in Pandora's box, after all the chaos in it had been released into the world. Without waiting too long for me to answer, he said very confidently, "Hope." Then he pointed to the angel standing on the devil and smilingly re-iterated, "It was hope."

David had by now stopped feeling blah. He had begun to develop the physical and psychic musculature needed to assert himself with his peers and to feel male despite having no father to affirm this. But his quicksand scene had set the stage for growth. It had quickened things, provoking change by the necessity to respond that it implies.

Case study: Emily

Seven-year-old Emily was a very bright and spirited child prone to phobias, rigidity, and at times aggressive outbursts. An intensifying phobia of dogs plus several incidents of biting her brother had brought her to therapy. Initially she made very elegant, functional sand scenes that had wonderful names such as "the world" and "the whole wide world" but despite her great delight in their creation these lovely scenes lacked vitality. Like her, they were rigid.

Then one day she made a scene that depicted a village by the sea, in which she placed a well. She poured water into it to make it more well-like and then dug into the softened sand until she had made a tunnel to the sea. She was entranced by the connection she had made from land to sea and also by the discovery that something solid could become liquid, and she began to combine sand and water to make a soupy mess. She took a bucket and made a batch of soupy sand in it, and then proceeded to play with it in a variety of ways, as a very young child might. She had never before made messes in her life! She had always played neatly, even as a young child, and her parents had been pleased with her tidiness. They needed my support to make room for a messier, louder but hopefully happier child, which they were able to do. Emily was in a trance-like state as she made her soupy sand and poured it into the box. She forgot about the storyline, the very clear position her characters were placed in. She could have played this way for hours, but the impact this brief play had on her was huge.

She came again after a few weeks and this time she again made a scene with a well to the sea. Rather than the dissolving play of her past session, she informed me that the well was used to clean out the seawater. It was a simple filtration system. She had invented a filter via the disintegration of her play. And the filter took hold in her as well. I had expected many sessions of disintegrative play, but she was very quickly able to tolerate the ebb and flow of the world around her and within herself. She was no longer afraid of dogs (she actually began to bring a stuffed toy of a dog with her to sessions). Prior to therapy she had been a loner in school, but now she used the word "we" when she spoke of her classmates—a subtle yet significant step.

Although Emily had not intentionally made quicksand or even called it that once she had done so, her sand had "quickened," it had liquefied and the end result was a provocation to change that she responded to.

Case study: Donna

Donna, a six-year-old dyslexic child, manifested the low self-esteem one would expect from a bright yet thwarted child in an advanced private school setting. As she watched the other children around her negotiate reading with ease, she slowly collapsed within. When I began to work with her she had begun to receive remedial help. Her initial scenes reflected a lack of confidence in her ability to do anything. She was sure that she would fail at making a successful scene, and the results were rather two-dimensional and flat. After a few sessions and lots of cathartic play with clay and monster drawings, her scenes began to get interesting. One day she came in and made the following multi-dimensional scene:

Two girls live together with their horses by a waterfall that flows into a large river. One of the girls goes to the edge of the river above the falls and tumbles in. She then gets stuck in a deep patch of quicksand that is in the river, right at the top of the falls. Will she remain stuck and drown or will she get unstuck and fall over the falls? The girl doesn't seem too upset. Her friend comes and throws her a rope and pulls her out of the quicksand/waterfall. They rush off on their horses together.

Donna was thrilled with her scene. She was relaxed and yet very engaged in the creation of it, hoping I would be both worried and delighted by its unfolding and the surprising storyline that ensued. As is often the case in attempting to retell the details of a scene, it is hard to explain how this scene "felt." It was as if by placing quicksand in the story, especially where Donna placed it, a whole new world of the imagination and the self had opened up within her and for her. Donna used this image of quicksand once she had actually begun to become unstuck in her life. It affirmed this new freedom, articulating it through her story and deepening the experience of it and herself as a result.

I did not see her again for several months. When I did, she seemed lighter and more self-possessed. She sat by the sand and created the exact same scene as she had when I last saw her, except that this time there was no quicksand at the top of the waterfall. Whatever function this image had served was no longer needed. She did seem to have become unstuck.

Perhaps it is best to think of quicksand as a symbol for the wonderful paradox that is the sandplay therapy process. It highlights the problem and brings to the surface the very energy that is needed to change the problem. Even when it is not used in an overt sense, it is present when the sandplay is alive and facilitating change. The sand can "quicken" by the child's simply deciding to have it so, or it can quicken without the child's conscious intention, simply because sand does that. Either way, once it has quickened, it offers what Carl Jung referred to as the "immediacy" of the moment. Its unique and largely fictional but mythic meaning makes it a perfect symbol for this immediacy, this sudden opening from which great things may emerge.

Reference

Bonsor, Kevin (2006) "How quicksand works" Accessed December 2007 at http://science.howstuffworks.com

Epilogue

Dennis McCarthy

In a world in which children from infancy on spend less and less time engaged in interactive, creative play, and in which even very young children are handed electronic devices rather than clay, paints, or blocks, the need to include these essential creative materials in our interactions with children becomes ever more important. It is through creative play that children grow, speak, and make connections to themselves and the world.

Although many children may still engage in structured physical expression, such as sports and dance classes, they are more restricted in the spontaneous movements that come on the playground or in the out-of-doors. The possibility for free movement needs to be a part of what we offer each child in our therapeutic setting. When children manipulate clay or paint, or draw or move spontaneously, aside from the normal health that this encourages, something potentially surfaces in them through these materials and experiences that can be transformative. The child who has been restricted in his or her self-expression may, simply by being allowed to do so, makes great leaps. When children are deprived of free play and negated in their imaginative powers, as so many children are today, even the day-to-day normal problems that arise in the process of normal development have no outlets for expression and resolution. A creative approach becomes ever more rare and ever more vital.

Children enter my office and see hundreds of monster drawings on the walls and it's a balm for them. These are not the monsters that the adult-run media bombard children with, but rather child-created visions of innate power, as well as visions of what it looks like when it is thwarted and runs amok in the child's psyche. But these visions still offer a resolution to the thwarted energy they contain by their very nature.

Children see the sandboxes waiting like blank canvases and they can hardly wait to engage with them, to reach in and manipulate the sand. Even the many children who have never played creatively innately know how to do so. Something in them surfaces in response to the material and they leap into action. They thirst for it. They recognize it for what it is, with little or no introduction. We may offer specific uses of each material or engage children in games or movement exercises that we suspect will be of help to them. But simply the presence in the play space of these non-verbal and non-specific forms begins the process of engagement and change. Simply the presence in the therapist of the knowledge that what needs to be said will be said in the spirit of play allows the child to know that here they will be truly seen and heard.

A five-year-old girl was recently brought for an evaluation. Her mother was seriously anorexic and in need of hospitalization, but wanted to make sure that her daughter could handle the month-long separation this would entail. She described her daughter as having recently begun to demonstrate intense anger and aggression. The child came into my office willingly but she largely ignored me at first. She ran round chaotically, showing signs of great distress. She snorted and bucked like a wild horse as she ran around. She announced that the stuffed animal she had brought with her was a "horse cat."

She periodically picked up small crystals that were lying on the floor, left by the last child, and tossed them randomly. She couldn't settle into play. She peeked through drawers and baskets but rejected everything including my efforts to engage her. I alternated between sitting by the sandbox and casually inviting her to join me there and moving randomly through the space with her, stopping where she stopped, joining with her in what felt like a mixture of fury, despair, and terror.

Although she was unable to do so at first, she eventually began to throw the small crystals into the sand rather than aimlessly round the room. At some point she sat by the sand and began to gather the crystals into a pile and then covered them up. "These are seeds," she announced. Later on, after more random movement, she returned with a bunch of small flowers and created a garden with them. The seeds had grown! She hid a giant centipede amongst the flowers and placed large spikes round the garden to protect it.

Once this was done she was able to sit at a table and work with clay, smashing it over and over again with a rubber mallet. In giving vent to her fury she calmed down. She asked me if she could borrow the mallet and some clay to take home with her. She would certainly need them in the coming weeks. She also spent time using the puppets, acting out a scene in which a witch had her head bitten off by a dragon again and again. This cathartic play, both the clay smashing and the puppet scenes, greatly reduced her anxiety and her fury.

The sand had focussed her and also gave a form to her feelings, allowing her to begin to express them. The crystals sank into the sand and then rose up as flowers. The centipede with its many spiky legs and the spikes placed round the garden seemed like apt images of what she must be feeling inside. But the seeds had sprouted into flowers. And the garden had been defined as such and defended.

It is hard to replicate with words the power of this largely non-verbal episode. There could be no words for this young child facing her mother's possible demise to express her emotions; her hopes and her fears. But the capacity to roam freely and experience herself in the free and sheltered space that was offered brought her to a place of at least temporary balance. So much was expressed, and in some small but significant way, resolved in our brief time together. The symbol of the horse cat, which was her actual intro-duction of herself to me, is of great interest, combining as it does two of the most common images of inner power that girls use. This too was unspoken really, at least in its inherent meaning to her, although it let me know that this child was a real dynamo, capable with support of negotiating the looming crisis in her family.

I offer in these final pages this child I saw only once, as in one short session she utilized all the many modalities described in the previous pages. She came to see me in the midst of my editing this book, affirming as I wrote and edited it the power of play and the non-verbal in all its forms, and how readily children may use these methods, each in their own unique way, to express the otherwise inexpressible. She expressed both the vulnerability that all children feel in the face of such trauma, regardless of how hardened they may seem, as well as resilience demonstrated in her play. We didn't speak about her mother's illness. We spoke non-verbally about how she experienced it, a much more difficult and important thing for a child to attempt to articulate, and an even more important thing to attempt to do. Perhaps if she were to continue coming we might someday talk openly in simple terms about her fears and her anger. But for now it was enough for her to share her chaos and rage and also to find some sense of safety in her flower garden.

The imagination is a seemingly endless wellspring from which children may draw the resources to express themselves and to face life in all its aspects.

From the 40,000-year-old cave paintings at Lascaux to the images drawn by children awaiting death in concentration camps during the Holocaust as well as those shared by the authors in these pages, it is the imagination that allows us to speak about the unspeakable and then to go forward into life.

Contributors

Jenny Bates, LCSW

Jenny Bates was born and raised in rural England, the daughter of medical parents and the grand-daughter of an emminent psychoanalyst. From an early age she has been interested in matters of the psyche, spirit, and healing. After completing a B.Mus. at Edinburgh University, she went on to train as a music therapist at the Guildhall School of Music in London. Subsequently, she received training in Advanced Music Therapy Studies under the tutelage of Dr Nordoff and Clive Robbins. After moving to New York City she worked at the Mother Centers, in childcare, group facilitation, and training, and also trained as a Dream Group leader under Dr Montague Ullman.

She received a Masters in Social Work at Adelphi University and worked with emotionally disturbed children in various settings on Long Island and New York City and later in upstate New York. Currently, Jenny is working part-time in private practice, specializing in play therapy, in New York State. She has received training in dynamic play therapy, which encourages the use of multiple and integrated modalities, such as bioenergetic play, music, imaginative play, sand tray, clay and paint, and storytelling. Her practice as a Buddhist also informs her approach to clinical work.

Jenny has published variously—chapters on music therapy and dream work, and in the *East Coast Sand Play Journal*.

Noëlle Ghnassia Damon, LCSW-R

Noëlle is a certified EMDR practitioner with a holistic psychotherapy practice in Kingston, NY. She has been working with adults, children, and families since 1978 in a variety of settings, ranging from community-based crisis intervention programs to mental health clinics. She utilizes a dynamic combination of strength-based modalities that involve the mind, body, and spirit to help her clients discover and explore their inner wisdom to heal old wounds and resolve disabling core beliefs. She specializes in the treatment of traumatic stress and has extensive experience of treating clients of all ages, and families of all configurations. She has provided trainings, authored articles and presented her work at regional conferences. She is currently a member of the East Coast Sandplay Therapy Association, the Child Psychotherapy Project, EMDRIA (Eye Movement Desensitization and Reprocessing International Association), the regional American Red Cross Disaster Relief Mental Health Team, and the Crisis Care Network.

Patti Knoblauch, PhD

Dr Patti Knoblauch is formally trained as a psychologist and school psychologist, and currently maintains private practices in Warwick and Kingston, NY. Her work is also influenced by her studies in sandplay, shamanism, poetry, meditation, and movement. She has been working with children for over 25 years.

Rena Kornblum, MCAT, ADTR, DTRL

Rena Kornblum, executive director of Hancock Center for Dance/Movement Therapy Inc., Madison, Wisconsin, has over 25 years of professional experience as a dance/movement therapist. She obtained a Masters in Creative Arts in Therapy from Hahnemann University and is a member of the Academy of Dance Therapists Registered. She has been on the faculty at the University of Wisconsin-Madison for over 20 years. She developed the children and family program at Hancock Center for Dance/Movement Therapy. She initiated an in-school program in which she provides therapy sessions for children dealing with trauma and abuse, as well as violence prevention classes for entire classrooms. Rena has written a book called *Disarming the Playground, Violence Prevention Through Movement*, published by Wood 'N' Barnes Publishers, and edited two training videos by the same name, all of which describe her prevention curriculum in detail. Rena has been doing workshops and trainings around the country and internationally on her work, and is published in several books. She was recently selected to receive the 2002 Wisconsin Dance Council Research and Journalism Award and the 2005 Wisconsin Alliance for Arts Education Distinguished Service Award. She is registered and licensed in the state of Wisconsin to practice psychotherapy specifically through the expressive arts therapies.

Brenda Lawrence, LCSW-R

Brenda Lawrence is a licensed clinical social worker and has worked with children and families for over 30 years; first as an early childhood educator, and as a play therapist since 1990. She has supervised other therapists in sandplay therapy and co-led a year-long training program in dynamic play therapy. She has had numerous articles published in the *East Coast Sand Play Journal*. She is currently working as a consultant to the Education Department on the island of Anguilla in the West Indies, providing play therapy and family therapy and co-leading parenting classes. Brenda is also an accomplished clay artist.

Claire LeMessurier, MA, LCMHC, ADTR

Claire LeMessurier is a member of the Academy of Dance Therapists Registered and a licensed clinical mental health counselor, who has worked with children and families for 20 years. Since 1999 Claire has helped initiate and develop services for children ages birth to six, in her role as regional coordinator for Vermont's Early Childhood and Family Mental Health program, Children's Upstream Services, known as "CUPS." Claire is in her tenth year as an adjunct faculty at Antioch University, New England for the Master's Program in Dance/Movement Therapy and Counseling. She presents locally and nationally on movement and early childhood mental health issues.

Ilka List, PhD, MFA, DA, RCAT

Dr Ilka List is a New York State licensed art therapist with a doctorate in Art and Art Professions, with a focus on the healing possibilities inherent in a deep, personal connection to the natural world. Her research demonstrates that ongoing experience in nature affects the cognitive and emotional development of children in a positive way. Profoundly interested in the relationship between outdoor experience, sandplay, and emotional health, she has developed a therapeutic garden around her office and home. She has worked with children for over 35 years, as parent, art educator, environmental educator, and summer camp director. She has been in private practice for the past 12 years as a psychotherapist working with sandplay, dramatic play, art, bioenergetics, and including encounters with animals, plants, and their environs in all of these methods. Ilka works with children, families, and couples.

Susan Loman, MA, NCC, ADTR

Susan Loman has been the Director of the Masters Program in Dance/Movement Therapy and Counseling at Antioch University, New England since 1987 and serves as Associate Chair in the Department of Applied Psychology. Professor Loman has served as the Chair of the Education Committee for the American Dance Therapy Association (1995–1999) and has been on the editorial board of *The Arts in Psychotherapy* since 1997. Considered an expert on the Kestenberg Movement Profile system, Professor Loman has written numerous articles, co-edited three books and taught the system in Germany, Italy, Switzerland, South Korea, Argentina, England, and the Netherlands, as well as throughout the US.

Dennis McCarthy, LMHC

Dennis McCarthy is a licensed mental health counselor and play therapist working with both children and adults. He is Director of Metamorfos Institute in Kingston, New York, which offers trainings and supervision for professionals, as well as yearly workshops for personal growth in Greece. He has worked as a therapist for 33 years, pioneering a dynamic approach to play therapy which combines Jungian and bioenergetic theory. He has described this approach in numerous articles in journals, including *Psychological Perspectives*, *Quadrant* and the *East Coast Sand Play Journal*, as well as in a book published by Jessica Kingsley Publishers in 2007, entitled *If You Turned into a Monster: Transformation through Play. A Body-Centred Approach to Play Therapy*.

Michelle Rhodes, LMSW, ATR-BC

Michelle Rhodes is a clay artist and art psychotherapist in Gardiner, NY and New York City. In her private practice, known as "Deep Clay," she sees children, teens, and adults and leads "Dreamfigures," a women's clay art therapy group. Her approach integrates archetypal psychology, Jungian thinking, Buddhism, traditions with current developments in psycho-analysis, and researches into the workings of the brain. She holds graduate degrees from Lesley College (expressive therapies) and Adelphi University (social work), and is currently in psychoanalytic training at the Institute for Expressive Analysis in New York.

Nancy Mangano Rowe, PhD, REAT

Nancy Rowe is Assistant Professor at the Institute of Transpersonal Psychology in Palo Alto, California, as well as a licensed creative arts therapist and mental health counselor in New York State. She is also a registered expressive art therapist. She develops curriculum and teaches courses in transpersonal psychology, creativity, spirituality, CA and eco-psychology and has presented workshops and seminars throughout the United States and in Europe. She is on the board of the International Expressive Arts Therapy Association.

Subject Index

abandonment 39, 46, 76
abuse, sexual 23, 49, 51–3, 104–6
ADHD (attention deficit and
    hyperactivity disorder) 130, 134
aggression
    emergence and containment 54–7,
        66, 94–7, 127, 147, 148,
        152
    inner-directed 146
Aikido 120
alcoholism 18, 20
amygdalae 61, 133–4
anger 24, 35, 52, 56, 103, 105–8,
    111, 119, 152–3
    failure to express 111
    paternal 137–8
    release 35, 56, 105–8, 119,
        152–3
archetypal
    energies 122, 126
    symbols 117, 121, 122
archetypes 122, 126
autonomy 101, 106

battacas see encounter bats
bioenergetics analysis 60
blocks,
    building 81, 91, 93, 151
    loosening through sandplay 70,
        133, 143
body-centered therapy 135
boundaries 27, 28, 34, 52, 55, 90–1,
    96, 98, 103–4, 129
building blocks see blocks, building

catharsis, play and 149, 153
chaos 18, 69, 127, 148, 152–3
chaos, harnessing 18, 148, 152–3
chickens, therapy with 82–4
child abuse 46, 50
Christianity 19
clay
    and alchemy 35
    modeling 20, 27–44, 60, 63, 81,
        90–1, 95, 99, 149, 151–3
clingy children 90
complex trauma 50–1
    see also child abuse
    see also domestic violence
consciousness 89, 92, 145
container, therapeutic 18, 103, 114,
    118, 120, 128
    see also containment, therapists
containment 55, 56, 82, 143
    see also aggression, emergence and
        containment
creation myths 144

creativity 17, 18, 25, 27, 33, 42, 56,
    62, 69, 72, 81, 87, 91, 94,
    99–100, 104, 118, 148, 150
crystal symbol 15, 152–3

dance 30, 33, 45–59, 61, 111–14,
    84, 89, 100–3, 105, 107–9,
    119, 138, 141, 151, 156–7
dance/movement therapy (DMT)
    45–57, 100–14,
death, effect on children 86, 93, 116,
    147, 154
defense systems 12, 16, 28, 110,
    133, 136–8, 143
depression 146
domestic violence 46, 50, 102
    see also violence
    see also child abuse
dragons
    puppets 153
    symbols 15, 74, 85–6, 147, 148,
        153
drawing strategies 63, 77, 110, 114,
    118, 123–5
dreams 12, 25, 116–17, 143–4

ego 10, 15
EMDR (Eye Movement
    Desensitization and
    Reprocessing) 130–42
emotions 58, 25, 27, 45, 46–8, 53,
    55, 57, 77, 79, 100, 107–8,
    119, 123, 130–2, 135–7, 153
    expression of 27, 45, 107–8, 119
    and health 25, 48, 77, 134
    non-verbal 62, 119, 123, 130–2,
        135, 153
    out-of-control 27, 79
    physical expression 46–8, 53, 55,
        57, 107
    stuck 147
empathy, non-verbal 46–7, 50, 57
encounter bats 60, 66
energy 12, 38, 62, 96, 102, 105,
    107, 115, 119, 121–6, 128,
    130–2, 135, 138, 143–4, 147,
    150–1
    discharge 138, 147
    thwarted 12, 62, 151
    transformation 122, 124–6, 147
    turning inwards of 121
environment 25, 47, 51, 56, 60, 80,
    86, 91, 93, 107, 110, 120–1,
    125, 134, 136
    negative growth
    non-verbal 121
    protective 25, 51, 56, 120–1, 136

    see also holding environment
Erikson, Erik 101, 105–6, 109
expressive arts therapy 58, 62,
    115–29, 135

falling 13
fathers
    hospitalization 102
    loss of 18, 20, 146–8
    mentally ill 54–7, 66, 94–7, 127,
        147, 148, 152
    sexual abuse 104
    weak/sick 52
Fear 13, 20, 60–2, 101, 111–13,
    130–2, 136–41
    see also phobias
form/formlessness 27–8, 36,
    117–25, 144
Freud, Sigmund 110
"frozen procedural memories" 132–3
frozen states 68, 73, 132–3

games 12, 18, 20, 25, 72, 84, 111,
    130, 136–7, 152
garden, and therapy 70, 76–82,
    152–3
gestalt 106, 114
goodness 17, 37
grief 37, 116, 131, 137, 147
grounding 19, 87, 102, 107, 112
guilt 101, 106
gut feelings 28–9

health 18, 20, 25–6, 45, 47, 54–7,
    74, 78, 90, 91–2, 96, 98–100,
    105, 120, 132–4, 151
    and emotion 25, 57, 74, 132
    and imagination 90, 92
    parental 105
hideout 81–2
holding environment 51, 55, 56,
    120–1, 136
Holocaust 154
horse symbols 67–8, 97, 150, 152–3
hyperactivity 54, 130

If You Turned into a Monster 116
illness 48, 52, 54, 107, 153
imaginative play 65, 91, 118, 155
impulsivity 104
Individual Education Plan (IEP) 99
individuality, expression of 15, 42
individuation 116–7
infantalization see regression
inner world 9, 77, 81, 137
instigators, therapists see therapists, as
    instigators

integration 17, 25, 100, 106, 116, 121–2

jumping 55, 60, 68, 102, 105
Jung, Carl 6, 7, 9, 10, 17, 116, 129, 150, 157

Kalff, Dora 17, 74, 116, 121, 128
Kestenberg Movement Profile (KMP) 54, 58, 101, 114
Knill, Paolo 118

labyrinths 13
language 11–15, 45, 54, 72, 97, 119, 122, 128, 130–3, 135–6, 141
Lascaux 154
latency 91
leaping 13, 60, 63, 80
learning disabilities 134
Lowen, Alexander 137
Lowenfield, Margarat 87

mandalas 19
McCarthy, Dennis 17, 116–17, 123
media 9, 25, 151
    internet 14
    television 14, 63, 80, 110
    television, effects on children 14
memories,
    pre-verbal 45, 135
    repressed 36, 132,
    trauma 45, 51, 131–2, 134,
    unprocessed 132–3,
metaphor 11, 12, 16, 35, 76, 78, 82, 86–7, 103
monster drawings 63–6, 71, 123–5, 149, 151
monsters 32–3, 40, 68, 72, 147, 151
    and sandplay 147
mothers 95, 97, 99, 105, 106, 108–10, 119–20, 122–3, 127–8, 131, 137–8, 141, 146–7, 152–3
    abuse 119, 131, 137–8, 141
    hospitalization 95, 152–3
    overly protective 105
    weak/sick 108–10, 152–3
muscular blocks, chronic 12
mutism 60–72
myth 13, 117, 122, 144, 146, 148, 150

National Child Trauma Network 51
nature 76–98, 145
non-verbal expression 10–11, 15–17, 20–3, 25, 45–6, 48, 53–7, 74, 100, 102, 104, 109, 113–14, 116–17, 120, 123, 130–1, 135, 152–3

Pandora's box 148
parent–child relationship 51
parents,
    boundaries 81
    guilt and remorse 14, 90
    neglectful 49
    of selective mutes 61–2
    self-understanding 90
    separated or divorced 23, 131
    of special needs children 48

supportive 24, 38, 90, 137
Phobias 148
places, safe 139
play fighting 60
play therapy 60–2, 66, 74, 89–90, 115–17, 120, 124, 135, 150
play
    cathartic 56, 149, 153
    disintegrative 149
    imaginative 65, 91, 94, 118
    interactive 138
    joyful 47
    symbolic 116–17, 122, 128,
ponds, therapy with 70, 76–85
protected space see space, safe
psyche 35, 92–3, 117–18, 121, 151,
psychic
    bonds 14
    energy 122
    fragmentation 23
    structure 27, 148
psychospiritual 120, 128
puppets and puppetry 60, 63, 72, 153

quicksand 143–50

rage 55, 144
rebirth 93, 97
regression 13, 34, 52, 54, 97
    using clay 34
re-parenting 51–4
rigidity 14, 16, 49, 52, 61, 72, 74, 76, 83, 138, 148
rituals 9, 52, 53, 63, 118, 120
Rogers, Carl 101
Rogers, Natalie 118–19

Sand, Water, Silence 125
sandplay 17–20, 23, 25, 26, 60, 74, 75, 87, 93, 115–17, 119–22, 125, 126–9, 135, 144, 150, 155–7
    crystals 15
    and depth of box 17–18
    and depth of the sand 17–18
    dragons in 15, 147, 148
    and energy release 126
    and "finding the treasure" 23, 26
    and form/formlessness 144
    and movement 127
    and projection 121
    and quicksand, see quicksand
    symbolic nature of 25–6, 122
    and transformation 116–19, 122, 128
    and volcanoes 144
Scaer, Robert 134
school difficulties 18, 24–5, 55–6, 61, 65, 68, 70–4, 84, 90, 99, 101, 110, 127, 130, 134–5, 146, 149
self
    emergence of 18, 25, 29, 45, 126, 150
    inner and outer 19–22, 133
    integration 45, 52, 57, 106
    repressed aspects of the 23
    sense of 16, 24, 87, 100–1, 133
    symbols of 26
    true 16, 25, 45, 117, 137

self-actualization 47, 116
self-awareness 11
self-regulation 45, 48, 51, 55, 57
sexual abuse 23, 49, 51, 104–5, 144
shadow 118, 121
Shapiro, Francine 131
Shiva 147
siblings 61–2, 67, 90, 97
sleep disturbance 61, 131, 138
snake symbol 37, 42, 127
space, safe 103–5, 114, 128
    see also environment, protective
    see also hideout
    see also tremenos
spirituality 19, 68
stories 38, 47, 71, 89, 95, 96, 106–7, 109, 116, 122, 124
stuckness 11, 56, 79, 144, 146–7, 150
symbolic play 17, 23, 116–17, 122, 128
symbols 10, 11, 17–19, 23, 25–6, 76, 81, 84, 109, 114, 117, 122, 125–8, 135, 145, 150, 153
    Christian 18
    of healing 10
    see also dragon symbol
synchrony 102

tantrums 61, 108, 109
temenos 120–1, 126
    see also space, safe
therapists,
    as containers 18, 87
    as instigators 15, 17, 76, 152–3
    non-verbal roles 12, 25, 74, 76, 100–5, 121, 128, 131
    roles of 11, 12, 45–57, 76, 100–5, 115, 121
    and transformation 76, 119
    as witnesses 18, 90, 109, 120, 127, 152
trampolines 63, 68
transformation 11, 14, 25, 58, 74, 94, 116, 119, 121–8
    and environment 121
    and healing 74, 128
    and movement 121–8
    and sandplay 25, 122
    and symbolic play 94, 116, 119, 128
    see also change
turning inwards 29

unspeakable 10, 12, 23, 87, 109, 135, 154

violence 46, 50, 58, 61, 102, 104, 107, 156
violence, domestic 46, 50, 102

war 50, 70
wholeness, sense of 26, 91, 109, 116, 118, 121
Winnicott, D.W. 17
witness, therapists as, see therapists, as witnesses

Author Index

Adams, M. 50
American Dance Therapy Association (ADTA) 100

Barron, L. 146
Bernet, W. 110
Bonsor, K. 145–6
Brett, E.A. 131
Bromfield, R. 47
Brooke, S.L. 47
Buelte, A. 54
Burnett, F.H. 78–9

Chaiklin, S. 47
Clements, J. 122
Cook, A. 51

Dalby, J. 101
Dumouchelle, D. 145

Eberhard-Kaechele, M. 47
Erikson, E. 101, 105–6, 109

Foley, F. 47

Goodill, S. 48

Harvey, S. 47

Jacobson, E. 111

Kalff, D. 17, 74, 116, 121, 128
Kestenberg Amighi, J. 46, 50, 101
Kestenberg, J.S. 46–7, 50, 54, 57–9, 101, 114
Knill, P.J. 118
Kornblum, R. 48, 101, 156

Lending Halsten, R. 101
Levine, E. 116–18
Levine, P.A. 138
Levy, F. 47, 102
Lewis, P. 51, 53, 58, 114
Lewis, Penny 51
Lohn, A. 47
Loman, S. 47, 50, 101
Loughlin, E. 48
Lowen, A. 137, 142
Lowenfeld, M. 87

Mandelbaum, D. 121
Markell, J. 117, 121–2, 125–7
McCarthy, D. 17, 116–17, 122–3

McNiff, S. 43, 117–18
Meekums, B. 48
Merman, H. 47
Metzner, R. 121
Moore, C. 101

Newlove, J. 101

Ostroff 131

Perls, F. 106
Perry, B. 52

Rogers, C.R. 101, 108, 116
Rogers, N. 116, 118–19
Ryce-Menuhin 122

Sandburg, C. 89
Sandel, S. 47
Santostefano, S. 82
Scaer, R. 134
Shapiro, F. 131–2
Signell, K. 121–3
Singer, J. 122
Sobel, D. 81
Sossin, M. 48, 101
Stern, D. 48
Stone, H. 106
Stone, S. 106

Taylor, J. 116
Tortora, S. 47, 56
Tortora, S. 47, 56

Utah Geological Survey 146

van der Kolk, B.A. 132, 134

Winnicott, D.W. 56, 59

Made in the USA
Lexington, KY
01 March 2010